D0446951

Praise for

The Music Lesson

"Victor Wooten has been doing things on the bass that nobody dreamed of, and we bass players can't help but hunger for some insight into what inspires him and how he does it. Here, as in his Music, he surprises us and gives us more depth than we expected, more of himself than many would dare. This is his journey, his mystical quest, not merely to play the bass but to fully encounter and understand Music itself."

—**Tony Levin, world-class bassist, Peter Gabriel Band**

"Wooten takes readers on a firsthand journey of his own musical self-discovery. Through his warm, humorous narrative—and with the help of some larger-than-life, guru-vy guides—Wooten reveals the laws of sound, vibration, rhythm, and creation in ways that help unlock the musical being in each of us."

—**Chris Jisi, senior contributing editor, *Bass Player* magazine**

"Read a chapter and change your playing. Read the book and change your life. This little book will inspire you to grow as a musician and a better person . . . Lacing the book with imaginative metaphors and unlikely comparisons, there's more wisdom contained in these pages than most musicians will ever learn in a lifetime."

—**Tony Rogers, guitar instructor, 95 North recording artist**

"A masterpiece of a book written by a master musician. Illuminating, motivating, riveting, and honest, it's a book you can't put down, one that you'll want to read over and over again . . . I feel it is destined to become one of the most important 'instruction' books of the new millennium. It's the best I have ever read."

—**Bob Franceschini, saxophonist, composer, and arranger**

≽THE≼
MUSIC LESSON

A Spiritual Search for Growth Through Music

VICTOR L. WOOTEN

BERKLEY BOOKS, NEW YORK

THE BERKLEY PUBLISHING GROUP
Published by the Penguin Group
Penguin Group (USA) Inc.
375 Hudson Street, New York, New York 10014, USA
Penguin Group (Canada), 90 Eglinton Avenue East, Suite 700, Toronto, Ontario M4P 2Y3, Canada
(a division of Pearson Penguin Canada Inc.)
Penguin Books Ltd., 80 Strand, London WC2R 0RL, England
Penguin Group Ireland, 25 St. Stephen's Green, Dublin 2, Ireland (a division of Penguin Books Ltd.)
Penguin Group (Australia), 250 Camberwell Road, Camberwell, Victoria 3124, Australia
(a division of Pearson Australia Group Pty. Ltd.)
Penguin Books India Pvt. Ltd., 11 Community Centre, Panchsheel Park, New Delhi—110 017, India
Penguin Group (NZ), 67 Apollo Drive, Rosedale, North Shore 0632, New Zealand
(a division of Pearson New Zealand Ltd.)
Penguin Books (South Africa) (Pty.) Ltd., 24 Sturdee Avenue, Rosebank, Johannesburg 2196,
South Africa

Penguin Books Ltd., Registered Offices: 80 Strand, London WC2R 0RL, England

THE MUSIC LESSON

The publisher does not have any control over and does not assume any responsibility for author or third-party websites or their content.

Copyright © 2006 by Victor L. Wooten.
Cover design by Weimanewman.

"Let It Be" copyright © 1970 by Sony/ATV Tunes LLC.
All rights administered by Sony/ATV Music Publishing,
8 Music Square West, Nashville, Tennessee 37203.
All rights reserved. Used by permission.

All rights reserved.
No part of this book may be reproduced, scanned, or distributed in any printed or electronic form without permission. Please do not participate in or encourage piracy of copyrighted materials in violation of the author's rights. Purchase only authorized editions.
BERKLEY® is a registered trademark of Penguin Group (USA) Inc.
The "B" design is a trademark belonging to Penguin Group (USA) Inc.

PRINTING HISTORY
Vix Boox editions / October 2006, March 2007
Berkley trade paperback edition / April 2008

Berkley trade paperback ISBN: 978-0-425-22093-1

An application to register this book for cataloging has been submitted to the Library of Congress.

PRINTED IN THE UNITED STATES OF AMERICA

20   19   18   17   16   15   14

Acknowledgments

Thanks to everyone at Penguin Group (USA) for publishing this book. Special thanks go to David Shanks, Norman Lidofsky, Leslie Gelbman, Susan Allison, Howard Wall, and Shannon Jamieson Vazquez. Thank you all for helping me achieve this dream.

There are many people who deserve credit in making this book a reality. All of U have taken part in my life knowingly or unknowingly in a way that has allowed me to become who I am. Whether U know it or not, U are a contributor to everything that I do.

This book is but one aspect of our endeavors together. I would like to thank U all for reading, proofreading, editing, advising, teaching, suggesting, criticizing, complimenting, putting up with, and helping me in some way or another, or not. It is all very much appreciated.

Special Thanks, Kisses, and Hugs go to:

My wife, Holly, and my kids, Kaila, Adam, Arianna, and Cameron, for loving, teaching, and inspiring me and for helping me to be a better me. I Love U!

My parents for teaching me about Life; My brothers Regi, Roy, Rudy, and Joseph for teaching me about Music; Paul Hargett and Rod Taylor for countless hours of help, editing, ideas, advice, and inspiration;

Danette Albetta, Steve Bailey, and Dave Welsch for continued friendship, guidance, help, and support;

All the members, crews, and supporters of The VW Band and Béla Fleck & the Flecktones;

My Music teachers—too many to mention—for sharing your gifts and her gifts with me;

My Nature teachers Tom Brown Jr., Charles Worsham, Richard Cleveland, Seth Recarde, Hilary Lauer, Colleen Katsuki, Jon Young, and others for awakening me to a new world and for showing me another way to see;

All the participants of the Bass/Nature Camps and Bass at the Beach for allowing me to experiment on U;

Richard Bach, Neale Donald Walsch, James Twyman, John Mc-Donald, Genevieve Behrend, and others for your inspired writings;

Kay Roberson, Denise Pilar Yver, Jennie Hoeft, Michael Kott, Sam Hunter, Jonathan Chase, and all who have helped and inspired in a special way;

And a big THANKS to my musical instruments for allowing me to express through them.

A Very Special Thanks goes to Michael and to Music for allowing me to write about them.

Thank U!
I Love U All!
Peace!

Victor L. Wooten

WARNING

Everything in this book
may be
all wrong.
But if so,
It's
all right!

Contents

Truth? What is truth? . . . And by the way,
if I always tell you the truth, you might
start to believe me.
—Michael

Grace Note

I believe that Music, herself, had something to do with you holding this book. What does that mean, "Music herself"? I once asked myself that same question.

I've been playing the bass guitar since I was two years old, but I started playing Music before that. The youngest of five musical brothers, I was welcomed into a unique world rarely seen by outsiders. It is a mystical musical world where, it seems, all are allowed to visit but only the chosen are allowed to remain.

Whether you play an instrument (or not), this world awaits you. How to get there is up to you. There are no directions given. My mom used to give hints when I was younger. She would say to my brothers and me, "You are already successful; the rest of the world just doesn't know it yet." I will put that into musical terms. "You are already musical; you just don't know it yet."

When I was younger, my brothers were like my extra parents, guides, and teachers. Actually, they are still that way to me. But now that I'm older, I understand the value of what they *didn't* teach me. I also understand their reasons for occasionally and strategically saying *nothing* when I asked a question. Under their guidance, I was allowed, and sometimes forced, to figure things out on my own. Thus, at an early age I became my own teacher.

In my forty-plus years of performing, I have come to a few of my own ideas about who and what Music really is. In my videos and at my clinics and camps I have begun to share some of these ideas. Some of them took courage to talk about openly. My friends kept telling me that these ideas needed to be voiced and that people were ready to hear it. They urged me to write a book. I knew that they wanted an instruction book. That's exactly what I *didn't* want to write.

Instruction books are often sterile and viewed as the author's authoritative viewpoint. They steer the reader down a narrow road toward a destination not of their own, but one set forth by the author. This is not a road I want anyone to travel.

Also, I wanted to separate the information from myself. In other words, if the information raised a question, I wanted the reader to question the information, not me. That's another way of saying that I didn't want to have to defend what I wrote. For example, how could I explain to someone that Music is real, female, and you can have a relationship with her? I can't prove it—that's something you have to discover for yourself.

Like one hand clapping, a one-sided relationship never works. It is clear to me now. For a relationship to work efficiently there must be equality in every way. Both parties must give to each other, take from each other, respect each other, love each other, and listen to each other. Only recently did I begin a complete relationship with Music. Previously, the relationship had been one-sided. Once I allowed Music to play a part in the relationship, things changed drastically. Of course I took from Music, but I always gave Music my best. At least I thought I did. My mistake was that I never really listened, not in a truthful way.

Here's what I mean. I listened to Music in the past but only in a one-sided way. I only listened to what I wanted to hear, not what Music had to say. It was as if I only wanted to hear my own opinion. Have you ever had a conversation where you didn't really listen to what the other person had to say? Of course you have. We do it all the time. We are usually so anxious to say the next word or phrase that we don't fully listen to what anyone else is saying. We feel the need to get our point across—the need to win. That doesn't cultivate a good relationship. It won't work with Music either.

Music exists inside each one of us. An instrument offers different forms of expression and allows others to hear how musical you are, but you don't have to play a note to be musical. I know that Music is not found in my bass guitar. It cannot be found in any instrument. My understanding of that has changed my Music and my relationship with her. No longer do I try to create her. I feel her and I listen! I know that I *must* listen to her for our relationship to be complete.

A friend once told me, "An instrument laid on the ground makes no sound. It is the musician who must bring Music forth, or not." Notice, he did not say that we must *create* Music. There is a difference.

In a few pages, you'll meet the man who introduced me to a whole new way of looking at Life. Many ideas were brought forth and walls were broken down under his tutelage. I may have never met Music without his guidance. He helped me become the musician and the person that I am today. Yes, there were others who helped along the way, but I must credit this one person for helping me find, once again, that magical musical place I had somehow forgotten.

To my friends: This is the book you've been waiting for. It's probably not what you expected but believe me, what you asked for is here. It's up to you to find it.

Remember when I said that Music, herself, had something to do with you holding this book. Well, she had everything to do with it. You're not sure how to feel about that, are you? You have reservations. No worries; so did I. Trust me and keep reading. We'll help U out; Music, me, and Michael.

Enjoy.

The Beginning

"Boy, do I have a lot to learn!"

There is nothing new about this statement, but the story I'm about to tell you may have you saying the same thing by the end. You can resist, as I did, but if not, it will only take you a moment to find a whole new world awaiting you, one you never before knew existed. Plus, resistance wouldn't stop him.

I'd been a musician for a long time. Well, let me change that right away; I'd played the bass guitar for a long time, about twenty years before I met him. Yet it wasn't until I met him that I learned the difference between playing the bass and actually being a musician, and better yet, the difference between being a musician and being musical. I thought I knew a lot about music already. I even thought I knew a bit about life, but what happened over the next few days proved to me that I was just a babe in this world.

I also thought I would never tell this story for fear of ridicule. At least, that's what I always told myself, but I actually knew it was because I wasn't sure if this story actually happened. And if I didn't fully believe it was real, how could I expect anyone else to? Who would believe me anyway? I mean, I never found out who this guy really was or where he came from. The more time goes by, the more I start to think that maybe, just maybe, he came from my imagination, from some unused portion of my mind, where he's now gone back to live. I can still hear him knocking around in there much of the time. It's as if he's constantly rearranging the furniture. I can hear his voice ringing in my mind saying, "Real? What is real? And tell me, what importance does reality have anyway? Did you learn from the experience? Now, *that* is important!"

He was a strange man, unlike any other music teacher I'd ever had. There was really nothing ordinary about him. He stood about six foot three with long, straight black hair that hung down past his shoulders. His facial features were distinct, yet in a way that made it hard to tell where he was from. He appeared to be part Native American and part . . . something else.

I've yet to meet another person with eyes like his. They were powerful. They were also as crystal clear as a Colorado mountain stream. When he would lecture me, standing nose to nose, as he often liked to do, the transparency of his eyes allowed me to look as deeply into them as he did into mine.

Also, on any given day, his eyes seemed to change color. One day, they would be bright blue. Another day, they would appear green, and yet another, they appeared brown. I never knew what caused it, but it was a great device for grabbing my attention.

Not only could I tell from his eyes that he was a healthy man, but also that his body was incredibly strong. Like a fine tool used for whatever task he chose, his body never seemed to falter or tire. Though I often saw him run, jump, gallop, and climb, I never saw him break a sweat. How he managed to stay so trim and fit, even though he ate and drank whatever he wanted, was a mystery. To him, a meal was a meal, and it didn't matter what it was or from where it came.

He also used his eyebrows as a tool. He could control his eyebrows better than most musicians could control their instruments. He could get a point across without speaking a word, just by wiggling one or both of his dark eyebrows.

His mannerisms were unpredictably quirky, and his clothes were always the type that drew attention, yet he never ever seemed to worry about what other people thought about him. Just about every time I saw him, he had on a different outfit. His shoes, when he wore them, were either an unnamed brand of boots or a pair of old worn-out sandals.

I almost hate to admit it, but I actually miss the little irritating qualities about my eccentric friend. He was the most, how should I say it, "free" person I've ever met. He wouldn't hesitate to strip off all his clothes, hop a fence, and jump in for a quick refreshing skinny dip in a private, *off limits*, outdoor swimming pool. Although he was always polite enough to ask me if I wanted to join him, hopping a fence naked in the middle of November for an illegal swim was not my type of fun. He possessed many of the qualities I would like to have, and I envied him for being able to do these things with seemingly no concern, worry, or embarrassment.

Having an opinion without being opinionated was a gift of his. How to do that remains a mystery to me. I know now that he just wanted me to think, to use my brain.

Answering my questions with a question was an important part of his teaching method. That frustrated me many times, but it made me think for myself. I'm sure that's all he wanted. I'm not sure if he ever outright lied to me, but I know that he frequently stretched the truth. Whenever I questioned him about it, he would answer with, "Truth? What is truth? And tell me, what importance does truth have anyway? Did you learn from the experience? Now, *that* is important. And by the way, if I always tell you the truth, you might start to believe me."

That confused me, as I always thought I was supposed to believe my teachers. I guess I was wrong. I can still see the sly smile on his face every time he knew he was totally confusing me.

Confusion seemed to be my natural state when I was with him, especially in the beginning. I recall him saying, "Music, like Life, and like you, is one entity expressing itself through its differences." My puzzled look let him know that I didn't understand. "Music is one thing," he continued, "but it wouldn't exist without its parts. You couldn't play a chord without different notes. Change a note, change the chord. Life is no different, and neither are you. You are expressing yourself in Life by choosing different notes all the time.

Learn to be conscious of your note choices and Life will respond with the proper chord or, in other words, Life will respond accordingly." I didn't know what to say. He just smiled.

He loved to laugh. I remember telling him about an invention I once saw called *The Lick Blocker*. It was a flat piece of board that attached to your wrist while you played guitar. It was supposed to block the audience from being able to view your hand, thus keeping them from being able to steal your licks. He laughed for a full ten minutes when I told him about that one. "I'm glad I ain't normal," he would often say.

"Sharing is one of the most important tools needed for personal growth," he once told me, also stating that many people never come to understand that point. He said that many of us try to hoard our knowledge in order to stay ahead of everyone else. I understood that completely because I used to use the same method. Somehow, I think he knew that.

It didn't take long for me to realize that I was learning more than just music. We rarely talked about it, but in the few days that we were together, he taught me more about life than anyone else ever has. "Music, Life, Life, Music: What's the difference?" I could hear him saying.

I remember criticizing him for leaving my car door unlocked. He asked me if I believed my mother whenever she would tell me that "all things happen for a reason." I told him that I did. "Listen to her, then," he responded. "Change your vibes. Stop creating reasons for your car to get broken into." I had to think about that one for awhile.

Vibrations were an important concept to him. I guess 'concept' is not the best word to use. I could tell that vibrations were important to him because he talked about them as if they were alive. His approach to music was the same, and he came alive whenever he talked about it. He seemed to think that all things were made up of vibrations, especially music.

"All things are in motion," he once told me, "and although a thing may appear to be stationary, it is always moving. This motion may change, but it will never cease. All Music ever played is still playing." I'd never thought of it like that. Whenever he mentioned the word "Music," he said it with a specific clarity I didn't have. It was as if I could feel the truth of the word vibrate whenever he spoke it.

He even told me that thoughts were vibrations. I had to think about that one for a long time too. I had no way of disproving him, and believe me, I would've if I could've, but when I thought about the way a lie detector works, measuring subtle changes in vibrations from the mind and body, I figured that he might have a point. He always had a point.

When I asked how he knew all that stuff, his immediate response surprised me. "A better question is: How come *you* don't know it? All knowledge that ever existed, or ever will exist, is already out there in the air. All you need to do is tune in to what you want to know."

He loved to talk about the power of the mind. "All things have a mind," he would often say. "Even an acorn holds, in its mind, a picture of the whole tree. If this were not true, how could the tree ever show up? Do you think that your mind is any less powerful than an acorn's? Pictures or Music held in the human mind are bound to come forth. They have to! That is the law! Learning to use the mind is the key to all possibilities."

His bold statements kept my mind spinning. I guess he was secretly teaching me how to use my mind because he never asked me to write anything down. Years passed before I ever realized that I'd taken no notes on what he'd said, or even one photograph of the man. There was nothing except my memory to document any of the experiences I'm about to relate. And speaking of my memory—well, I forgot what I was gonna say.

The only physical evidence that remains from his visit are twelve handwritten measures of music. He quickly wrote them out one night while we were playing together at my house. He said that they were a gift from Music. At first, I thought that he meant to say, "a gift *of* music," but he always said what he meant. The measures were supposed to contain all of the elements he'd been showing me. We played those few measures together as a duet, but he said that, one day, I would be able to play the whole piece by myself. I'm still waiting for that day. I've never shown it to anyone. Most people would just say that I wrote it, and maybe I did.

I don't know what happened, but one day, I just decided to write the whole story down for myself. It was while I was writing these notes that I was convinced, by some unknown force, to share this experience with you. He would've said that I convinced myself, but I'm sure it was his voice that kept interrupting my thoughts asking, "Who are you writing this for?" I'm still unsure what the answer to that question is, but since you're reading my words, maybe I'm writing them specifically for you.

Like me, you may be wondering who this guy really was, where he came from, and where he is now. I don't know if I can accurately answer any of those questions. Sometimes I think that he came from another planet. Maybe he was a wandering, retired college professor or even a mystic from the Himalayas. He's probably roaming around somewhere searching for his next impressionable victim, someone else's mind to screw around with.

Maybe all the above is true. I've learned not to rule out any possibilities. The one thing I know for sure is that what he taught me, no, showed me, about Music and Life is as refreshing to me now as it was when I was hearing it all for the first time.

So, in following his example, I will share my experience with you. Once it enters your mind, you're on your own. What you do with it is up to you. I won't promise you complete accuracy or complete honesty, and don't waste your time trying to figure out which part is truth and which is not. It's what you get out of it that's important. "Truth is your decision anyway." And as he told me over and over again: "I want you to think for yourself."

"Boy, do I have a lot to learn!"

Groove

*You should never lose the groove
in order to find a note.*

I'd been working in the Nashville music scene for many years and not once had I seen him. I was a known player around town and had played in many bands and no one had ever mentioned his name. Although I hoped to make a decent living playing music, keeping my head above water on a consistent level was always a struggle, and the present struggle was rapidly getting the best of me. Maybe that's what brought him out.

I was out of work but determined not to take a job waiting tables like so many musicians in town were forced to do. My landlord had just called to remind me that the end of the month was only a few days away, and with no gigs lined up, I was in no rush to return his call. My girlfriend, well, no need to lie about that; I didn't have one.

As much as I tried, I could never seem to break into the recording session scene. The few sessions I'd done never generated any return calls, and whenever I lost a gig with a club band, I rarely knew why. I was a good bass player—not the best, but good—so I couldn't understand why anyone wouldn't want me in his band.

Without a steady gig, and not knowing what to do, I decided to start practicing more. I didn't like practicing (and still don't), but I knew that I had to change something. It was either magically get better, alter my playing style, or move to another town and start all over. Realizing the gravity of my situation, I decided to practice.

Did I mention that I hate practicing? I never know what to practice or why I'm practicing it. I also get sleepy in the middle of the process.

So there I was at home, painstakingly working on scales and modes and not knowing why. I just knew that my previous teachers had told me to do so. All the books I'd ever read said the same thing, so that's what I was doing.

I was at my lowest point emotionally because I wasn't getting anywhere with my playing and I wasn't satisfied with my current playing situation. My home life and my love life, well, my whole life in general, wasn't in the best of shape.

The rain beating down on the metal siding of my duplex, coupled with the monotony of playing scales, was lulling me to sleep. It was during one of my sleeping sessions, I mean practice sessions, that I first met him; or, more accurately, when he first showed up. And that is exactly what he did. He showed up, uninvited! At least, I thought he was uninvited. He had a different story. He said that I'd actually called him. I'm still confused by that statement, but somehow, for some reason, there he was in my house.

I have no idea how long the stranger had been standing there looking down on me. The fact that he was completely dry when it was raining outside made me wonder if he'd been there awhile. The strangest part of all is that . . . I didn't want him to leave.

From my position on the couch, he appeared quite tall and mysterious. He was wearing a blue NASA-style jumpsuit and a black motorcycle helmet. And even though his eyes were hidden, I could feel them penetrating deep into my mind as though he was looking for the proper place to begin.

"How'd you get in here?" I asked, startled, half asleep, and wondering why I wasn't angry at his intrusion.

"You asked me to come."

"I did?"

"Yes."

"But how'd you get in here? Who let you in?"

"You did."

"Oh really! Did I give you a key?"

"I don't need a key."

"Who are you?"

"I am your teacher."

"My teacher?"

"Yes."

"My teacher of what?"

"Nothing."

"Nothing? Well, then, what are you supposed to teach me?"

"What do you want to learn?"

"Lots of things. What can you teach me?"

"Nothing!"

"What do you mean 'nothing'?"

"Exactly that, nothing."

This was typical of conversations to come, but at that time, I didn't know what to make of him and I needed a straightforward answer.

"You have to do better than that. You showed up in my house unannounced; I think I deserve some kind of explanation."

Tilting his head, he looked at me through the face shield of his helmet and replied, "I teach nothing because there is nothing to be taught. You already know everything you need to know, but you asked me to come, so here I am."

"But you said that you're my teacher."

"Yes, I did, but try to understand. 'Teacher' is just a title. I cannot teach you because no one can teach another person anything."

"What do you mean by that?"

"You can only teach yourself. Until we live in a day where I can physically implant knowledge into your head, I can teach you nothing. I can only *show* you things."

"What can you 'show' me?"

"Anything."

"Show me everything then," I replied.

"That would take a while. It might be easier if we pick a subject."

"Okay, how about music?"

"Perfect! Music! Shall we begin?"

I didn't know if I was ready to begin anything with this character. I already told you he was wearing a blue jumpsuit and a black motorcycle helmet (yes, he was still wearing the helmet), but did I mention that he was carrying a skateboard under his left arm and a burlap bag over his shoulder? I imagined him riding his skateboard down the street, through the rain, in his getup.

I didn't know what I was getting myself into. I also couldn't tell if he was really serious or not. For all I knew, he could've been there to rob me. But I didn't think so. There was a lot I didn't know, but I decided to play along anyway. There was an intriguing quality about him, and I wanted to know more.

"Wait a minute. If you're not a teacher, what are you? What should I call you?"

"Michael. Call me Michael," he answered as he removed his helmet and offered me his hand.

I remember his bright blue eyes as hypnotic. They had an immediate effect on me. Somehow, I sensed they could see beneath the surface, and I was fearful of what he might uncover. I struggled to stay in control.

Not bothering to move from my reclined position on the couch, I allowed his hand to dangle in the air. Asserting what

I thought was dominance, I responded in a cocky tone, "Okay, Michael, what can you teach me about music?"

"Nothing. I already told you that," he answered, retracting his hand. "I tried teaching many times before. Once as an Apache medicine man in New Jersey and twice as a Yogi in India. I even tried teaching while flying biplanes in Illinois. This time around, I am living the laws of Music. Some may call me a teacher, but I don't teach; I show."

This guy was full of . . . well, something. I couldn't quite make him out. *Is this a joke?* I thought. *Is he an actor? He said that he is living the 'laws of Music.' What does that mean? Music has rules, that I know, but laws? It's not like we're talking about the law of gravity or the speed of light or—*

"Science," he commented, interrupting my thoughts. "Music is bigger than you think."

"Science," I said to myself. That's exactly what I was gonna say. How did he do that? Coincidence? Must've been.

"*Mu*," he continued, "is an ancient word for 'mother,' and *sic* is just an abbreviation for the word 'science.' So, put together, *Music* means 'the mother of all sciences.' So you see, Music is important. I can show this science to you if you'd like. Is it something you would like to see?"

Even though he was talking like a crazy man, he had my undivided attention. But I didn't want to give in too soon. I also figured that since it was my house, I should be the one asking the questions. I reclined even more and laced my fingers behind my head. Next, I put my legs in a crossed position and tried to act cool. He gave a slight smile as if he was ready to counter my every move.

"What instrument do you play?" I asked.

He turned and took a seat in the chair across from me. Laying his skateboard in his lap, he tucked his hair behind his right ear and took a breath before responding.

"I play Music, not instruments."

"What do you mean by that?" I asked, losing my imagined control of the conversation.

"I am a musician!" he answered. He placed his hand on his chest to emphasize his point before gesturing at me. "You are just a bass player. That means you play the bass guitar. A true musician, like me, plays Music and uses particular instruments as tools to do so. I know that Music is inside me and not inside the instrument. This understanding allows me to use any instrument, or no instrument at all, to play my Music. I am a true musician, and one day, you too shall be."

He spoke with confidence, and I was trying to find a way to strip him of it.

"Are you saying that you can play any instrument?" I asked.

"Of course I can, and so can you! It is this knowing that separates us. A true writer can write using a typewriter, a pen, a pencil, or anything else that he chooses. You wouldn't call him a pencil writer, would you? Your understanding that the writing utensil is just a tool allows you to see past it and into the truth of what he is—a writer. The story is in the writer, is it not? Or is it in the pencil? Your problem is this: You have been trying to tell your story *with* a bass guitar instead of *through* it."

I liked what he was saying, and that bothered me. Trying to hold on to my resistance, I struggled to find the holes in his argument. The more I lay there thinking about what he'd said, the more interested I became in Michael and his ideas, and the less interested I became in finding the holes.

He definitely had a unique way of looking at things. Yes, he had shown up uninvited, and I probably should've been upset about that. At first, I was, but suddenly, I wanted more. I wanted to hear him talk. If he could help me become a better bass player, I was ready to let him. Maybe.

"Do you know what it means to be a bass guitarist?" he asked.

The question was a strange one. I didn't know how to answer, so I didn't.

"The bass guitar is the honorable instrument," he declared.

"What do you mean?"

"It is understated and underappreciated, yet it plays the most important role. The bass is the link between harmony and rhythm. It is the foundation of a band. It is what all the other instruments stand upon, but it is rarely recognized as that."

I struggled between getting sucked in by his words and trying to keep my dominance over the situation. He was winning.

"The foundation of any building has to be the strongest part," he continued, "but you will never hear anyone walk into a building and say, 'My, what a nice foundation.' Unless the foundation is weak, it will go unnoticed. People will walk

20

all over it and never acknowledge that it is there. The Life of a true bass guitarist is the same."

"Wow! That's pretty cool! I never thought of it that way before."

"Why not?" he asked.

I was disappointed in my outburst. I didn't want to show my enthusiasm just yet, so I regained my composure and answered more calmly. "I don't know. I guess no one ever taught me music this way before."

"Therein lies your first problem," he stated.

"Problem? What do you mean by that?"

"You still think that you can be taught."

Not knowing what to say, I stared at the floor in silence for a long while. The stranger remained quiet as well, allowing me time to digest his words. I wasn't sure what he was talking about. I mean, we're all taught at some point in our lives, aren't we? I can remember taking music lessons as a kid, and I definitely had a teacher. I'd even taught music lessons myself when I first moved to town. Realizing, again, that I'd totally lost control of our dialogue, I found myself getting worked up.

I was reclined on the couch with my bass in my lap, trying to figure out something to say. He was sitting there in front of me in what I would eventually think of as "his chair." I could tell he was looking directly at me, but I dared not look back. For some reason, I didn't want him to know how uncomfortable I was.

Remember: It had just been a few minutes since I was . . . uh . . . practicing. My mind was in a daze, my thoughts were racing, and there was a stranger in my house.

I reflected on grade school and all my teachers and all the summer music camps I'd attended when I used to play cello. How about all the music books or even the metaphysical books I'd read over the years? They were interesting, but none of them had prepared me for this.

Neither my mom nor my dad played a musical instrument, but they were very musical, more musical than some musicians I know. They sang in church and there was always a record playing on their stereo at home. They also helped spark my interest by taking me to concerts when I was young and supported my musical interest by offering to pay for lessons if I wanted them. I can't say they taught me how to play music, but they surely supported my decision to play. Hearing it around the house was such a major part of my childhood that it was like a second language to me.

"Language, that's good." Michael spoke out of the blue, as if reading my thoughts.

"What?" I replied in disbelief.

"Language, that's a good one."

"Wait a minute! Can you read—"

"Music?" he interrupted with a sly smile. "Of course I can. Can't you?"

"That's not what I was gonna say," I muttered.

Knowing where I was heading, he steered the conversation by asking, "Is Music a language?"

"I would say so."

"Then why don't you treat it like one?"

"What do you mean?"

"What language do you speak the best?" he asked.

"English," I answered.

"Are you better at English than you are at Music?"

"Much!" I answered, not knowing where he was headed.

"At what age did you get really good at English?"

"I would say by about age four or five I was fluent."

"And at what age did you get really good at Music?"

"I'm still working on it," I answered in total seriousness.

"So it took you only four or five years to get really good at English, but even though you've been speaking Music for almost four times as long, you're still not really good at it yet?"

"Well, I guess not," I answered, finally realizing his point. I hadn't looked at it from that perspective.

"Why not?" Michael asked.

"I don't know why. Maybe I just haven't practiced enough." I was frustrated by the question.

"How much did you practice English?"

"All the time," I answered, but then I thought about it. "Well, I didn't really practice English; I just spoke it a lot."

"Bingo!" he replied, "That is why you speak that language naturally."

"So, are you saying that I should stop practicing music?" I asked sarcastically, trying to regain some ground.

"I'm not saying that you should or shouldn't do anything. I'm just comparing the two languages and your processes of learning them. If Music and English are both languages, then why not apply the process used to get good at one of them to the other?"

Realizing I'd totally lost my ability to direct the conversation, I finally relaxed and gave in.

"How do I do that?" I asked.

"How *do* you do that?" was his reply.

I had to think for a minute, but I soon came up with an answer.

"Well, when I was young, I was surrounded by people who spoke English. I was probably hearing it even before I was born. So, since I've heard people speaking English every day of my life, it was easy for me to pick up because it was always around. How's that?"

"It's a start; keep going."

"Okay. Because I heard English every day, speaking it came naturally to me." I was talking more quickly and with more confidence. "It wasn't something I ever thought about. It wasn't something I ever really practiced. I just did it. I just listened to it and spoke it. And the more I spoke it, the better I got."

"That's brilliant! See, you do understand. I like the part about it coming naturally to you. I must be a good teacher," he said smiling.

"Comedian? Yes! Teacher? I'm not so sure," I retorted, joining in on the fun.

"How can we apply this approach to Music?" Michael inquired.

"I'm not so sure," I answered. "I am around music most of the time. It's hard to go anywhere without hearing some type of music playing in the background. So that part of it is similar to English, but I know that there's still something missing. There has to be something else that keeps me from being just as good at music as I am at English."

I thought for a moment.

"Oh, I know. I speak English every day. I'm always talking, but I'm not always playing. I don't play music every day. If I played my bass every day, I'd be just as good. Is that it?"

"Did you speak English every day when you were a baby?" he asked.

"Well, not exactly." Apparently there was more.

"Do you need to speak English every day to get better at it?" he asked.

"No, I don't."

"Then what's missing?"

"I don't know." My frustration grew. "Just tell me."

"Jamming!" he stated with a slight nod of his head.

"What?"

"Jamming," he repeated. "That is the missing element. When you were a baby, you were allowed to jam with the English language. From day one, not only were you allowed to jam, you were encouraged to. And better yet, you didn't just jam; you jammed with professionals. Just about everyone you communicated with when you were a baby was already a master of the English language. And because of that, you are now a master."

"A master?" I inquired.

"A genuine master," he confirmed. "The only reason you are not called a master is that everyone else is just as good at it as you are. Everyone is a master. Think about it. If you were as good at Music as you are at English, you would surely be considered a master. Would you not?"

"Oh my God! You're right!" Another unintended outburst. The words just leapt from my mouth, seemingly of their own free will. What he was saying made so much sense. I was surprised I'd never recognized it before.

"Thanks for the compliment, but please keep listening," the stranger continued. "There are only two elements that allowed you to become a master of the English language at such a young age. Only two: being surrounded by it, and jamming with it. That's it! English came quickly and easily to you, and from what you told me, you were also surrounded by Music, so it must be jamming that makes the difference.

"Imagine if we allowed beginners to jam with professionals on a daily basis. Do you think it would take them twenty years to get good? Absolutely not! It wouldn't even take them ten. They would be great by the time they were musically four or five years old.

"Instead, we keep the beginners in the beginning level class for a few years before we let them move up to the intermediate level class. After a few more years at that level, they may move up to the advanced level class, but they still have to work up through the ranks of that class before they are really considered advanced level players. Once they stay at that level for a few years, we turn them loose, so that they can go pay their dues elsewhere. Think about it. After all these years of training, you still have to pay dues. When it comes to learning a language, what does paying dues mean? How many dues did you have to pay while learning English?"

Michael had interesting things to say. Abandoning my need for dominance, I sat up on the couch. The only way I can explain it is that I wanted to get closer to what he was saying. I wanted him to keep talking, all day if he was willing, but he paused as if inviting me to say something.

"I see your point," I replied, "but not all of us have access to professional musicians. I can't just call up Herbie Hancock or Mike Stern and say, 'Hey, I'm coming over. Wanna jam?' So what now? What am I supposed to do if I don't have professionals to play with every day?"

"You could have chosen to be born into a family of professional musicians," he answered without a smile, making it hard for me to tell if he was serious or not.

"It's too late for that now," I replied.

"I guess so. There is always next time. Still, there are professionals you can bring here to you."

"Really now? How am I supposed to do that?" I wasn't following his logic.

"Who would you like to jam with?" he asked.

"Well, I've always wanted to play with Miles Davis," I answered with a smile. I was only half joking.

Placing his skateboard on the floor, he rode over to my bookshelf and pulled out a Miles Davis CD, as if he'd placed it there himself. I didn't think much about it then. He put the CD in the player, pressed *play*, and nodded his head toward me.

"What do you want me to do?" I asked.

"Play," he answered.

"What am I supposed to play?"

"What is Miles asking you?"

"What do you mean, 'What is Miles asking me?'"

"I thought you said Music is a language. Are you telling me that you can't understand what Miles is asking you to play?"

"Um, I don't know," I sighed. I was slightly embarrassed by the question.

He turned off the CD player and picked up my acoustic guitar, which was sitting in the corner being used as a coat rack. The guitar was an old, beat-up, pawn shop special that hadn't been played, or even tuned, for I don't know how long. It didn't even have a brand name. I called it a "Majapan" guitar because it was made in Japan. Years earlier, I had a pickup installed inside, but I rarely plugged it in. That guitar was unplayable, or so I thought.

He sat down, placed his foot on top of his skateboard, and without the slightest bit of hesitation, began to produce the most amazing sounds. The music that poured out from beneath Michael's fingers was astounding. It was . . . well . . . it was Miles Davis!

"Play," he ordered.

"What key are you in?" I asked as I picked up my bass.

Ignoring my question, he looked me straight in the eyes and repeated himself in a stern voice, "Play!"

I recognized the song right away. It was "So What" from the *Kind of Blue* album, but I had no clue as to the key he was playing in. I fumbled around for a while until I finally found it, and as soon as I did, Michael stopped playing.

"Where are you from?" he asked abruptly.

"Virginia," I replied.

Immediately, he started playing again as if he didn't care about my answer, but this time, he was in a different key.

"Play!" he instructed again.

"What key?" I repeated.

He stopped playing, this time asking me for my shoe size.

"Nine and a half," I replied, more than a bit confused.

"Play!" he commanded in a stronger voice, as he continued strumming the guitar.

I knew better than to ask for the key, so once again, I fumbled around until I found it. And, once again, as soon as I did, he stopped.

"What kind of bass is that?" he inquired for some unknown reason.

"A violin-shaped Univox. It's a copy of a—"

Not letting me complete my sentence, he spoke firmly.

"Why is it that when I ask you a verbal question, your answer is immediate and direct? But when I ask you this—" he started playing again in a different key, "you don't seem to know how to answer. Don't you know this song?"

"Yes, I do, but—"

"Well, what's stopping you? Play!" he nearly shouted.

"But I need to find the key first!" I tried to hide my frustration, but he sensed it, and didn't seem to care.

"Oh, I see. You can't play Music until you first find the key. Very elementary." He stood up and walked over to where I was sitting. I guess it was so he could talk down to me. "What do you need a key for? I didn't even need a key to get into your house. Do you think your listeners have time to wait for you to find the key?"

"Well, usually I know the key before I start playing," I responded with hesitation.

"Do you always know what you're gonna say before you start talking?"

"No."

"And does that stop you from talking?"

"Not usually."

"Okay, then, play!"

He sat back down and, again, started playing in yet another key. For the first time, he seemed a little irritated, which didn't make things any easier for me. I took a deep breath and jumped right in, playing along with him as best as I could.

I fumbled around trying to find the root note so I could figure out something good to play but quickly got frustrated and put the bass down.

"That was horrible," I mumbled.

"You could use some help, but we'll get there," he replied in a gentle voice. He was smiling now, as if pleased with me all of a sudden. "What were you thinking about when you were playing?"

"I was trying to find the right key."

"And you need to find the right key before you can play Music?"

"It helps."

"Why?"

"I need to find the right key so that I can play the right notes."

"I see. Notes are so important that all Music stops until you find the right ones?"

"I didn't say that."

"Yes, you did. You said it clearly with your bass."

"Well tell me, then; when should I find the right notes?"

"You shouldn't."

"I shouldn't?"

"No! Not at first anyway. There is something more important you should find first."

"And what is that?"

"The *groove*!"

"The groove? Wait a minute. So the first thing I should do is find the groove when I start playing?" That was news to me.

"No! You should find the groove *before* you start playing. It doesn't matter whether you know the song or not. If you need to, let a few measures go by while you figure out what the groove is saying. Once you find the groove, it doesn't matter what note comes out; it will 'feel' right to the listener. People generally feel Music before they listen to it anyway. If finding the key is so important to you, at least find it while you groove."

I wanted to say something, but I couldn't think of a way to prove him wrong. I just stared at him while I fidgeted with my bass.

"Forget about your instrument," he said, staring back at me. "Forget about the key. Forget about technique. Hear and feel the groove. Then allow yourself to become part of Music."

Still holding the guitar, he started playing again. He leaned forward and nodded. Realizing I was not going to win the staring contest, I closed my eyes and waited, trying to figure out what to do. I decided to give in and do what he had suggested—listen. I listened to the groove.

Then a strange thing happened. Listening to the groove allowed me to hear more of the music. All of a sudden, along with Michael's guitar part, I could hear the drums, then the piano. I could hear Miles's trumpet too. I could even hear myself playing the bass, even though I wasn't holding it yet.

As if he was listening to what I was hearing, he spoke, more softly this time, "Play."

Without opening my eyes, I picked up my bass and started playing. I don't know if the first note I played was the right one or not, but it surely sounded good. Really good. I was shocked. I didn't want to lose the feeling, so I kept playing. I was lost in the music. The thought of a blue-eyed stranger in my house was no longer an issue. I was jamming with Miles Davis!

I opened my eyes to see that Michael had stopped playing and had already put the guitar down. He was applauding me, yelling, "Bravo! Bravo!"

I was proud of myself. "How did I do that?" I asked.

"How *did* you do that?" Michael repeated, forcing me to answer my own question once again.

"I don't quite know, but it sounded good to me. I just grooved, I guess. I didn't think about the notes at all, but everything I played seemed to work."

"That's right. Everything worked because you grooved before you started playing," he added.

"Groove before I play." I resolved to commit this new concept to memory.

"I have a saying," Michael said, "and I think you should remember it. It goes like this: 'Never lose the groove in order to find a note.'"

"I like that, and I think I understand it. Are you saying that grooving is more important than playing the right notes?"

"Don't jump to conclusions prematurely. All the elements of Music are equally important, or not."

"The 'elements of music'? What are you talking about? What is that?"

"The elements of Music are the individual parts that make up Music as a whole. Many musicians like yourself struggle because you are not familiar enough with all the elements. You rely mostly on one or two of them when you play. Doing that is a great recipe for frustration. A musician like me, who appropriately uses all the elements, will be one of the greats even though he may not be aware of the fact that he is using them. Actually, it would be nearly impossible to become a great musician without using all of these elements."

What he was saying was interesting even though I didn't totally understand the concept. "Elements" was not a term I usually associated with music.

"Can you please tell me more about these elements and how to use them?" That was something I had to know more about.

He flashed a sly smile, leaned forward, and whispered,

"Why do you think I am here?"

Notes

If you stopped playing notes,
Music would still exist.

"Let's pretend that Music is made up of ten equal parts," Michael began. "If we were to take a few minutes to break Music into parts, we could come up with hundreds of different ways of doing it, but for the sake of argument, let's just say that it contains only ten different parts. Ten different elements that are all equal, or not."

"Michael, why do you keep saying 'or not'?" I asked.

"Because the choice is always yours," he answered.

"Okay, then, Michael, let's do it . . . or not!" I countered with my own smile.

His eyes widened and he gave me a "thumbs up" before continuing the lesson.

"Even though you didn't know the key, what you just played sounded good because you had most of the elements in balance. If you do that consistently, it won't matter if you make a mistake. It will fly right past the listener's ears because the Music will still 'feel' right." He raised an eyebrow. "Do you understand?"

"Yes, I think so. But can you tell me what each of the elements is?"

"I would rather you tell me. I'll give you the first one just to get you started, but you must give me the rest. You're already very familiar with the first one because it gets most of your attention when you play. We'll call the first of the elements *notes*."

"Yeah, now I realize that notes are the first thing I think about. What about the other elements?" I asked.

"What about them?" Michael continued, "If notes are just one of the ten elements, what would the other nine be?"

"How about melody or harmony?" I asked.

"Wouldn't those be included in the first category? Anything dealing with pitches we'll put into the notes category. That means harmony, melody, re-harmonization, scales, modes, chords, key signatures, relative majors and minors, and other stuff like that. What else besides notes can you come up with?"

"How about *articulation*?"

"Good one, that's number two. What else?"

"*Technique.*"

"Nice, go on."

"How about *feel*?"

"I like that one because it can be looked at in different ways. Most people think about feel as it relates to the groove, but that's just the obvious way to look at it. I can show you other ways of looking at feel. If you approach it from the angle of emotion, meaning how you feel when you play or how the listener feels and how you can affect that, then it gets interesting."

"That sounds cool," I said. "I'd love to learn more about that."

"It's up to you what you learn. I will show it to you if you'd like."

"Okay with me."

"Good! Feel, number four. What else?"

I paused, trying to think of more elements to add to our list. Michael allowed me to take my time. Just before I reached the limit of my frustration, he spoke.

"Can you hear me?" he whispered.

"What?"

"CAN YOU HEAR ME?" he yelled.

"Yes, I can! Oh, I get it, *dynamics*. That's the next element, right?"

"Works for me; five to go."

"How about *rhythm*?"

"Rhythm is perfect. It is an elusive element. It also lets us know that the elements are related to each other."

"How so?" I asked.

"Rhythm can be looked at as harmony slowed down."

"What do you mean?" He totally lost me with that comment.

"*A-440* means that a note vibrates four hundred and forty times per second, right?"

"Yeah, I understand that."

"If you keep cutting that number in half, 440, 220, 110, 55, etc., you will eventually get beats per minute. At that point, it's called rhythm. You see?"

"I do. Man, that's cool. I've never heard anyone talk about that before. And the best part is I think I actually understand it."

"Thinking is good enough for now," he said. "If we want to, we can combine rhythm with *tempo*. They are different elements, but for our sake, let's put them together. Cool with you?"

"Cool with me."

"All right, that's number six. What else?"

I sat there for a full minute trying to come up with something else to add. I was still trying to digest what had already been said, and it was getting harder and harder to come up with more elements. I knew they were there, but thinking of them was difficult. *It shouldn't be this hard*, I thought. My struggle made me realize that when I play, my thinking is quite limited.

"Can you hear me now?" Michael asked in a high thin voice.

"Yes," I answered, trying to figure out what he was getting at.

"How about now?" This time he used a low bassy voice.

I knew he wasn't trying to demonstrate pitch because that would be in the first category called notes. Then it hit me.

"*Tone!*" I yelled.

Michael chuckled. "You're slow, but you do get there eventually. Tone, number seven. Very good. Next?"

"How about *phrasing*?" I asked, almost immediately.

"Phrasing is a good one," he answered. "Most people only think of phrasing as pertaining to notes, but any of the elements can be phrased. We will look at this again, later."

He was right. I'd never thought of phrasing anything but notes. But how can you phrase tone or dynamics? The concept intrigued me. Michael interrupted my thoughts.

"Two more to go."

I sat there struggling for another couple of minutes before he finally broke the silence.

"The final frontier."

"What?"

"*Star Trek*, William Shatner. The final frontier."

"Oh. *Space.*" I finally got it.

"Right. Space, rest, not playing, very important! This is the underused but all-important element. Think about it: If there were no rest, all Music that was ever played would still be playing."

The thought of there being no rest was disturbing. Right about then, I was really appreciating the existence of that element.

"One more to go," Michael stated.

Once again, I sat in silence, thinking, until Michael helped me out.

"What are you doing when I am talking?"

"What? Oh! *Listening!* I get it! The final element," I answered.

"Very good. Now, we have ten different but equal parts of Music: *notes, articulation, technique, feel, dynamics, rhythm, tone, phrasing, space,* and *listening.* We could have made our list one hundred or one thousand elements long, but for now, we will stick with these ten. Is that okay with you?"

"They work for me."

"Good. Think about all ten of these elements and tell me this: When most teachers talk about music theory, which element are they usually talking about?"

I thought for a few seconds. "Well, 'notes,' I guess."

"Good, what else?"

I tried, but couldn't think of anything else.

"Notes," I repeated.

"That's right," he laughed. "Notes, pitches, and that's it! All the fuss about learning music theory, and now we see that most teachers only teach you how to use one tenth of the elements on our list! Their music theory only teaches you how to use notes, and it's only a theory! That's it! Nothing else! It doesn't teach you about dynamics, feel, tone, or anything else on the list, only notes! It should be called note theory, not music theory, because it doesn't teach you Music!

"You can't speak Music with notes alone, but you can speak Music without notes at all! I can program a computer to play notes, and it won't sound like Music! You need these other elements to make it complete! Without them, notes are lifeless! Music theory is shallow! Incomplete! It does not deserve all the attention it gets! But at the same time, notes *are* important."

Whew! That was the first time I'd heard him speak with such force. He sounded like he really had a point to prove. I didn't quite know what to say. I didn't even know if what he said was true. Michael was silently looking at the ground, so I decided to speak up.

"I think I understand your view on notes, so will you help me understand more about all the other elements?" I asked.

"Yes, we will look at all the elements individually. We've started already, but let's not leave the subject of 'notes' just yet. Let's dive in deeper. You ready?"

"Ready!"

"Here we go."

I didn't know what I was getting myself into. For some reason, I agreed to let this man 'show' me about music, and although he had some interesting ideas, I didn't know if he really knew anything about it at all. Had he studied somewhere, or was he making it up as he went along? I sat for a short while contemplating my dilemma when my thoughts were shattered by an outburst.

"Notes are overrated!" Michael shouted, slamming his fist into his open palm.

"Overrated?" I asked. "I get the sense that you have more to say about the subject."

A lot more as it turned out.

"Most musicians think that Music is made up of notes. They forget that notes are just a part of Music, and a small part at that. If you stopped playing them, Music would still exist. Think about that! The reason many musicians get frustrated when they start to play, especially when they start to solo, is that they rely mostly on notes to express themselves. There are only twelve notes. Imagine trying to speak a whole language using only twelve words.

"You see, for musicians, bass players especially, groove should be most important, but groove is not found in notes. It is found in the other nine elements. The other elements, put together, define the essence of groove. That is why, when musicians try to play by twelve notes alone, they quickly run out of things to say."

I knew what he was talking about, and I was definitely guilty of it. Most of my musical study had been dedicated to notes, which was why I usually had a hard time playing well. Everything I knew about groove, I'd learned on my own. No teacher or book ever really told me what it was. When I thought about it, I realized Michael was showing me that groove, for the most part, doesn't get equal attention.

I've seen many books teaching notes, but I've yet to see a book on rest, articulation, or tone. I realized that most of the other elements we listed were rarely taught. Most musicians had to learn them on their own. This was starting to get interesting. I was getting a glimpse into the vastness of music, which made me wonder why most teachers chose to confine it to twelve notes. I hoped Michael could shed more light on the subject.

"Many musicians," he said, "are afraid of those twelve notes. If they hit the 'wrong' one, they get scared and quickly leave that note in search of the 'right' one. That's what you were doing when you were trying to find the key. If you make friends with whichever note you happened to land on, it will give you directions to where you are trying to go.

"Most inexperienced bass players have to find the root before they can play anything else. That is a very elementary way of thinking. When I asked you to play earlier, you didn't listen to what you played. You only listened for the root, and when you didn't hit it on your first try, you jumped around blindly until you found it.

"Now listen," he instructed as he walked over to my cheap electronic keyboard. "There are how many notes in Western Music?"

"Twelve," I answered.

"How many notes are there in most of the key signatures we play in?"

"Seven."

"Correct. In any key, there are seven so-called 'right' notes which leave only five so-called 'wrong' notes. What this means is even if we don't know what key we are in and guess which note to play, we will be 'right' more than half the time.

"Look," he continued, pointing at the keyboard. "In the key of C major, the 'rule book' states that you're allowed to play the white keys only. But what would happen if you accidentally landed on a black key? Nothing, because if you look on either side of this 'wrong' note, what do you see?"

"A 'right' note," I answered proudly.

"Absolutely! You are never more than a half-step away from a 'right' note. Never! So, what are you so afraid of? You can't be lost. If you land on a 'wrong' note, just step off of it in either direction, and you are 'right' again. 'I once was lost, but now am found.' Even if I close my eyes and throw a dart at the keyboard, I will hit a right note more than half the time. 'Was blind, but now I see.'"

His way of looking at notes caused me to see them in a new way. If I was never more than a half-step away from a 'right' note, like Michael had said, my world would be much easier. That was a relief. Michael read my thoughts (perhaps literally).

"This is liberating, is it not?" he remarked. "The real beauty is this: If you use your ears and listen to that accidental note, you may find that it actually sounds better than the 'right' note you intended to play."

He walked back over to the guitar and started playing a simple groove. He looked at me, talking while he played.

"Don't be afraid of the notes; jump right in. All I want you to do is listen to whether the note is in the key or not. Just think 'in' or 'out.' If the note is 'in,' listen to it and realize where you are in relationship to the root. If the note is 'out,' slide your finger one fret in either direction, and *voila*, you are right again."

I picked up my bass and, without thinking, played the first note my finger landed on. It sounded horrible, so I quickly slid my finger down one fret. Michael was correct, I was now on a 'right' note, and it sounded good. I wanted to test his theory, so I played the same wrong note again, but this time, I slid my finger up one fret. Like before, I was on a 'right' note. It made me smile.

I also noticed something else. I wasn't sure as yet that it was really happening, so I repeated the process a few more times. I then found a different 'wrong' note to start on and repeated the whole process. What I noticed shocked me. I started to tell him what I'd discovered. Seeing the expression on my face, he spoke first.

"Go ahead; tell me."

It was difficult to explain, but I gave it a try: "I noticed that when I went from the 'wrong' notes to the 'right' notes over and over again, it made the 'wrong' notes gradually sound 'right.' The more I did it, the 'righter' the 'wrong' notes started to sound until they didn't sound 'wrong' at all anymore."

"Why?" he asked me. "Why didn't those notes sound wrong anymore?"

"Maybe it's because the 'wrong' notes are leading somewhere. Repeating the 'wrong' note allows the listener to know where it's going so that it begins to sound 'right.'"

I confused myself. It surprised me that Michael understood what I had just said.

"Very nice." He was smiling now. "I call this 'massaging the notes.' It's a great way to correct mistakes after they've already been made. I like to think of it as a way to change the past."

"I like that," I said.

"I've got a million of 'em," he responded in a comedic voice. "You can also play the 'right' notes so much that they start to sound 'wrong.' Overusing a note can sound just as bad as playing a 'wrong' note. Basically, every note has something to say. They all lead somewhere if you just listen to them. How you use them is the key. As I said before, the notes will tell you where they want to go. You just have to listen."

"I know that I don't listen that way," I commented.

"I noticed," he replied. "Many musicians study so much music theory that they only remember how to tell the notes where to go. They have learned to forget that notes are alive. I urge you to listen to the notes. They may have something to tell you."

I'd never thought about listening to notes that way, to see what they had to tell me. I'd always tried to tell the notes where to go, and most of the time they seemed to resist.

"Let me hold your bass," he instructed.

Michael took my bass and handed me the guitar. He asked me to play the same chords he'd been playing. Before I had to ask, he let me off the hook by telling me what they were—Gm to C7. The guitar didn't sound the same in my hands as it did in his, but I did my best. He asked if I could play and listen at the same time. I said that I could.

Michael started from the highest note on my bass and moved down one fret at a time, playing every note on the instrument. He then did the same thing in reverse starting from the lowest note and ending at the highest. It was simple, but against the chords I was playing, it sounded amazing.

I'd never heard that done before. I'd also never heard my bass sound that good. My old Univox, which I'd always thought of as "beat-up," suddenly came to life, and all he'd done was play a chromatic scale. I knew that many of the notes he played were not in the key signature and shouldn't have sounded that good, but somehow he made them all work. I was astounded at what I was hearing.

"Which of those notes sounded bad?" he asked with a confident smile.

"None of them did," I replied, still in shock.

"Why?"

"Because *you* were playing them and not me."

"The first truthful thing you've said all day. You graduate! Class over."

"No really, I don't know why all the notes sounded good. I guess it was *how* you played them that made them work."

"Right again. Now, how did I play them?"

"I don't know. I guess you . . ."

I couldn't think of an appropriate answer at first, and then it hit me. I had the answer and I knew it. It was so simple that I was surprised that I'd never thought of it before that day. I didn't even feel proud of myself for coming up with the answer because I should have known it immediately.

"You didn't just rely on the notes alone. You added in more of the other elements of music." I knew that I was right, so I answered with my own smile of complete confidence.

"Progress," I heard him whisper, almost to himself. "We are making progress."

For the next few hours, we played music together, often switching between bass and guitar. What he showed me was remarkably simple. Every once in a while he would use the keyboard to demonstrate something else about notes. His proficiency on that instrument was just as stunning as it was on the guitar and the bass. The only thing that surprised me more was the fact that, until that day, I didn't know that the keyboard still worked. Until that day, I wasn't sure if my brain still worked either, but I was starting to get it. I was actually understanding what the crazy man was showing me.

We massaged notes, listened to notes, directed notes, and just played notes until I was familiar and comfortable with all of them. He had me spend time with the chromatic scale, one note at a time, "listening" to what each had to say about the key we were in. Then he would change keys and have me repeat the whole process. Each note would say something different as the chord changed. That exercise was a revelation to me.

Another exercise involved playing notes randomly, without thinking of what I was going to play first. "Just play any note," he instructed. "Jump all over the bass as if you don't care." I was surprised at how hard it was to do. I had a difficult time not playing patterns. My fingers kept landing on top of the frets instead of in between them.

"Mistakes," he told me, "are just things we didn't mean to play. It doesn't mean they are 'wrong.' Some of the best Music I've ever played started out as a mistake. Mistakes usually throw us off because the note comes out before we think about it. We can't avoid making mistakes, but we *can* get comfortable with them, especially if we practice making them."

The thought of practicing mistakes was another strange

but interesting idea. I had no idea how I was supposed to practice that. Michael answered my thought.

"This 'random' exercise simulates making mistakes so that they no longer affect us negatively. If we learn to play random notes cleanly, playing any pre-thought note or pattern will be a piece of cake."

I was learning things I'd never learned before and it was exciting. My mind was open and receptive to everything he had to say. Well, almost everything. It was exactly what I needed.

"Play like a child with an air guitar," Michael advised. "A child playing air guitar never plays a 'wrong' note."

For the first time in a long time, I played like a child.

I loved it.

Articulation/ Duration

*Every time you move, and every time you play a note,
a piece of yourself is left behind.*

We played for hours, just the two of us having fun. I don't remember the last time I'd done that without expecting to get paid. Eager to learn more, I asked Michael to teach me about the other elements of music.

"Soon," he answered, "I have more to show you about notes first. Let's look at them in a different way before we call it a night. How we view notes provides a good example of how we view Life."

"How we view life? What do you mean?"

He played a *C* and a *C sharp* at the same time on the guitar.

"How does that sound?" he asked.

"Awful! It sounds like two notes clashing," I responded with a grimace.

"Very ordinary answer," he said matter-of-factly. "Now, if I take the *C* up an octave and play the two notes again, what does it sound like now?"

"Now it sounds pretty," I answered. "The *C* became the major seventh which is a key factor in making a chord sound pretty. That's cool."

"Correct. The rule book tells us that two notes played side by side, a half step apart, should clash and sound dissonant, but if we move the lower note up an octave, the same two notes sound pretty. Why is that? They are the same two notes, so how can they clash in one instance, and sound pretty in the next? There is a Life lesson in there somewhere."

Interesting, I thought. "So are you saying that situations in life which seem to clash may not be 'wrong' at all; they may just be in the wrong octave?"

"It is *you* who is saying that, but I do agree. Keep going with that thought."

"Okay, I've never thought about it before, but I'll give it a try. How about this? If we can learn to change our perspective and see negative things in a different 'octave,' we may be able to see the beauty in all things and in all situations."

"Bravo! I'll accept that. Very *articulate*, simple and to the point. All situations and all people contain beauty, but it is up to us to see it. When we don't see it, our immediate response is to blame, then change the outer thing rather than change our perspective or our octave. It is only when we change octave that we can see things as they really are. Then, and only then, can we make a positive change when and where it needs to be made."

Once again, I was learning new things about music and life. I was fascinated by the way he paralleled the two. I didn't know what I was getting myself into when I originally agreed to take part in this situation, but if he really meant it when he told me that he could "teach me nothing," he sure had me fooled. Even though I'd just met him, he was already the best teacher I'd ever known, bringing out parts of me I never knew existed.

"Here's another way to look at these two notes," he continued. "Let's say that we don't change the octave of the *C* or the *C sharp*. Let's just surround these two notes with other notes and see what happens.

"If you play a *B flat*, a *C*, a *D flat*, which is the same as a *C sharp*, an *F*, and an *A flat*, you have a *B flat* minor nine chord. Now the *C* and the *C sharp* sound good even though they are right next to each other and in the same register. People could learn a Life lesson from Music if they would just choose to see." He began to sing, " 'I can see clearly now the rain is gone.' "

"Johnny Nash," I responded, recognizing the lyric. "That's a beautiful song."

He nodded in agreement. "Also," he continued, "in the key of *B flat* minor, the rule book tells us that we are not allowed to play a *C sharp*, but when I play it, it sounds good to me. We're supposed to call it a *D flat*. Even though they are the same note, we can play one but not the other. It's all in the name, I guess. Rules!"

"They can be confusing sometimes," I added.

Michael told me that once the rules were thoroughly learned, they could be thoroughly broken. He said that the same was true with life's rules. (I eventually witnessed him break or bend rules many times. Most of the time I hadn't even realized what the rule was; I just knew that one or two of them were being broken.)

He also told me that the beauty of the world could be seen through music. "There is always beauty to be found, and it is necessary to find it in all things and in all people if real change is to be made in this world," he said. He seemed to think that what we see in life and what we hear in music are simply our choice and that when things start to look grim, that is when we really need to find beauty. I remember his telling me: "It is always easier to build upon this beauty than it is to pretend it is not there and try to create it from scratch." That is a comment I will never forget.

I've had many music lessons in my life, but never before had I experienced anything quite like Michael. None of my teachers had ever shown life through music in a way that I could clearly understand. Even though I didn't totally under-stand Michael, he made things clearer than they had ever ap-peared before, and he wasn't finished. He was just getting started.

He played two more notes on the guitar and asked me how they sounded. Again, they seemed to clash, but this time, I was afraid to say so. He could tell by my expression what I was thinking. Next, he played what sounded like two different notes. I could hear a slight wobble as they vibrated against each other. These two notes sounded better and I told him so. He told me that they were the same two notes. I didn't believe him.

"Those were the same notes?" I asked.

"Absolutely!" he responded. "I just articulated them differently the second time. I also held them a bit longer. Changing the *duration* allows your ear to hear and respond differently."

"Wait a minute!" I said. "You're telling me that the way you played the notes caused them to sound different? I mean, even the pitch sounded different."

Michael didn't respond. He just walked over to my bookshelf, pulled out another CD, and placed it in the player. With the remote in his hand, he sat down and looked at me in silence. I had no idea what he was up to or what his musical choice would be this time. The anticipation was starting to build. He just sat there, staring at me with his sly grin.

When he knew that I was uncomfortable enough, he pointed the remote and pressed *play*. The music that came out of the speakers shocked me. I didn't know who it was. It was a CD I surely didn't believe to be part of my collection. It felt like Michael was trying to torture me. The music was . . . well, it was bluegrass!

"I *hate* bluegrass music!" I cried out.

"All the talk about beauty, and that's all you have to say?" was his response.

"Well, that's the first thing that came to mind."

"What are you talking about?" Michael asked, pressing *pause* on the remote.

"Bluegrass," I said.

"No! You are not talking about bluegrass! You are talking about yourself!" Michael leaned forward as he spoke. His dark eyebrows nearly touched each other as he narrowed his gaze.

"Listen to what you are saying. 'I hate bluegrass music.' You are talking about you but blaming your lack of perception on this particular style of Music."

Even though he was right, I felt as though he was attacking me, and he didn't stop. He continued his assault.

"We do the same with people. All Music, like all people, contains beauty and a soul. For you not to recognize it is not Music's fault. It is *you* we are talking about! It is *you* who does not recognize! There are millions of people who love this Music. Are you here to tell me that all these people are wrong?"

"I'm not saying that they're wrong; I just don't like bluegrass music."

"Who are you talking about?" he asked.

"Me."

"Good! More progress."

Michael sat back and closed his eyes, smiling as if he'd just won a battle. Without looking, he pushed *play* and nodded his head at me. I started to pick up my bass so I could play along, but with his eyes still closed, he tucked his long hair behind his right ear and whispered, "Listen. Just listen."

I didn't know what he wanted me to listen for, but I figured that if I acted like him, maybe I could listen like him. So I leaned back and closed my eyes too.

After a few minutes, Michael spoke: " 'Blue Moon of Kentucky' by Bill Monroe. He is the father of bluegrass Music. Listen to the bass on this track. Can you play like that?"

"Of course I can. Country music is easy to play. *One—Five—One—Four—*, no problem."

"First of all, this is bluegrass; there is a difference. It is closely related to country Music, but it is also related to jazz. They're kissing cousins. You may not hear it yet, but you will one day. Some of the best improvisers on the planet play bluegrass, and playing it may not be as simple as you think."

Now, I admit that I hadn't listened to much bluegrass or country music in the past, so maybe he was right. I couldn't hear it. But there was one point I really felt he was wrong about. I knew this type of music was easy to play, no matter what he said.

It only took a few minutes for me to realize that, once again, Michael was right. He introduced me to the nuances of the music by asking me to pay close attention to how the bass player articulated each note in that particular song. There *was* much more to Mr. Monroe's music than I'd previously realized. I didn't know how to feel about that.

"Notice how each note starts and ends," he instructed. "Listen to the way he attacks each note and notice whether the notes are long, short, or in between. Recognize the Life of each note. Can you hear the beginning, middle, and end of each one? If he had articulated differently or changed the duration of any note, would that have changed the feel of the song? Listen."

Again, Michael sat back and closed his eyes, so I did the same. I tried to pay attention to the life of each note.

The song was in three-four. I noticed that the bass player was playing whole notes, except that he didn't let each note ring for its full duration. He would cut them off just before each downbeat. I also realized that if the notes had been any shorter, the song would have had a little more bounce, and if they were any longer, the song would have felt slower.

The relationship between the slow three-four time signature and Bill's rhythmic way of singing gave the song an interesting feel. Also, the attack of the acoustic bass felt different than an electric bass would have felt. How the bass player played each note helped dictate the feel of the song. It made me think of how I usually approached my notes. I rarely let them ring. I usually attacked them hard and fast. I thought about each note having a life, as Michael had alluded. Listening to the bass player caused me to realize that I rarely gave my notes enough air. But the most amazing thing was that in allowing myself to listen to Bill Monroe so deeply, I enjoyed his music, if only slightly.

I opened my eyes and noticed Michael staring at me. Stopping the music, he asked a strange question. "You ever read *Horton Hears a Who*?"

I didn't know what that had to do with anything, but understanding that Michael had his own way of teaching, I answered him, "Of course I have. Dr. Seuss."

"Do you remember what that poor elephant found on the little speck of dust?"

"There was a whole civilization living on it," I answered.

"Exactly!" he said, pointing at me. "Notes are the same. If you listen closely, you can find a whole world living inside each one. Notes are alive, and like you and me, they need to breathe. The song will dictate how much air is needed. There is no rule hard and fast, but usually, the sharper the attack, the shorter the sustain. The vice versa is also true.

"Now, here's what I want you to do this time. Breathe with the Music. Listen to the song one more time and take a breath with each note as the bass player plays. It will help you understand what I am talking about.

"After that, I want you to play along with the song, breathing with your own bass notes. If you change the length of your notes, you must also change the length of your breath. Do that and pay attention to what it does to you and to Music. Don't go to sleep tonight until you have done it at least twice. We will continue tomorrow. I will leave my bag here if that's okay with you."

Without waiting for a response, Michael put on his helmet, pulled down the face shield, turned, and walked out the front door, skateboard in hand.

For a time I just sat there staring at the closed door, reflecting on the many things the strange man had said. I'd already learned so much from him. It was hard to believe that we'd met for the first time earlier that day.

"Breathe with the Music," he had instructed. What did he mean? I'd never listened to or played music in such a fashion, but once I did as he'd suggested, things started to change. Breathing with the music caused me to hear it and feel it in a way I never had before. I could actually feel the notes mixing with my heartbeat. It was like a meditation. I don't know if it was my slow rhythmic breathing or what, but whatever it was helped me to begin to understand Mr. Monroe's music for the first time, and, I hate to say it, but I liked it.

That Michael: He was a sneaky character. At least ten minutes had gone by before I realized I was actually learning how to play a bluegrass song. In order to play along while breathing with my notes, I had to learn the music. He tricked me into doing something I would've outright refused to do if I'd been asked. I knew that he must've been smiling right about then. I was.

As I got up to go to bed, I saw Michael's bag lying on the floor as if it had fallen off of the arm of the chair. Sticking halfway out of the bag was a book. I tried to leave it alone, but what I could see of the title made me curious.

The Science and Art of—I couldn't see the rest, but I really wanted to. I wasn't sure whether I should remove the book from his bag or not. I didn't want to go through his stuff, but the book was already halfway out and my curiosity was getting the best of me; I didn't know why, but it was. Just peeking at the title wouldn't be wrong, right? I tried to distract myself by going into the bathroom to brush my teeth, but it didn't work. *The Science and Art of*—'Of what?' I asked out loud.

Okay, just a quick look, I told myself. I practically ran from the bathroom to the bag. I guess I was secretly hoping for something different, but the bag was still lying there in the exact same place with the book poking halfway out.

Michael is so peculiar, I thought, trying to come up with an excuse. *I may never see him again anyway. Plus, he might have left it here on purpose, just for me to find*. I convinced myself a quick glance would be all right.

The Science and Art of Tracking, by Tom Brown Jr. I was confused. It was a book on animal and human tracking. I couldn't quite fathom what Michael was doing with a book about footprints, but it looked interesting. Tracking was an interest that I had held since my childhood days of pretending to be a spy, but I never really learned much about it.

I am familiar with a trumpet player named Tom Brown, and quite frankly, even though I love his music, I'm not sure if I would've read a book about him. But Tom Brown Jr. the tracker? *Hmm, let's see.*

About an hour later, I forced myself to stop reading. Not wanting Michael to know I'd touched his things, I put the book back using my best James Bond spy skills. "He'll never know," I whispered to myself as if someone might hear.

With my mind tired and full, I went to sleep and slept hard, for a little while anyway.

I awoke to the sound of banging on my front door. I looked at the clock: five fifteen *a.m.* I don't know any musician who gets up at five fifteen in the morning, so I rolled over and tried to go back to sleep. Then I heard his voice.

"Let me in! Let me in! I can't find the key." I could hear him laughing through the door.

I got up and opened the door. I had to admit that Michael was funny, but I wasn't going to encourage him by cracking even a faint smile. I gave him my best sleepy look. He didn't seem to care. He waltzed right in wearing a pair of brown shorts, a forest green shirt, large black boots, and a tan safari hat. Around his waist was a small pack, and he was carrying his skateboard under his left arm.

"Time to go," he said.

I couldn't imagine going anywhere that early except back to sleep. "Go where?" I asked.

"Tracking, but we have to move quickly. The sun is just starting to rise, and it will be at the perfect angle soon. Did you read the book?"

"Uh, no, I didn't. What book?" I didn't plan to lie. The words just popped out of my mouth. I also didn't know what to think. Was he baiting me with the book, or were my spy skills that lacking?

He looked at me and smiled one of his now-familiar Cheshire cat grins. Picking up a shirt from the floor, he threw it at me and turned toward the door. "Let's go."

Slowly starting to wake up, I put on the shirt and followed him. "You got room on that board for me?" I asked with a chuckle.

"It might take longer, but we would see much more," he responded in all seriousness.

We hopped in my car and drove west on Interstate 40. Nashville is the type of city that attracts people from all over the country, especially musicians. It's not too big or too small. This allows people from larger cities, such as Los Angeles or New York, to sell their small homes, move to Nashville, buy larger ones with lots of land, and still not be too far away from city life. I like it because you only have to drive a few minutes to be surrounded by trees.

I've always loved spending time in the woods, but my musical life never allowed me the opportunity. At least, that's what my excuse had always been. I dreamed of someday owning a log cabin in the woods.

We drove down a beautiful winding road in Cheatham County that was flanked by rolling hills on the east and the long narrow Harpeth River on the west. The scenery was beautiful at that time of the day. The low morning sun shining through the trees and reflecting off the remaining white oak and hickory leaves filled the air with magic.

The dark rippling river slithered and twisted like a snake tempting us to take a bite of the forbidden fruit that lay just on the other side. I was instructed to park the car on the right side of the road near one of the bends in the river. Then we walked up a steep, rarely used trail to the top of Mace Bluff.

Mace Bluff is a tall hill covered in scrub pine and cedar trees that overlook the river. The ground cover—mostly poison ivy—is so thick it acts like a barrier protecting the mountain. Few casual strollers would risk a trek through it.

At the top of the hill is a low sitting flat rock with a carving in the center. This ancient carving is known as the Mace Bluff Petroglyph. Researchers have wondered about the carving for years but have never come to a conclusion as to what it is. All they know is that its origins are Native American and that it is hundreds of years old. All I know is that the panoramic view from the top of the bluff is breathtaking.

Michael stood with his eyes closed and his hands raised above his head. He took three slow deep breaths. I didn't know what I was supposed to do, so I just stood there watching. I could tell that this was a sacred place to him, and I waited for him to tell me about it. I especially wanted to know about the carving in the rock. Instead, when he was finished breathing, he sat down on top of the carving as if it weren't there and pointed across the river.

"Look," he said, "through the trees. That is an area called Mound Bottom. It was a sacred place used by Native Americans hundreds of years ago. Some of those natives still come back to that place today."

I didn't know if he was talking about living Native Americans or spirits from the distant past. I hadn't seen many Native Americans in Nashville, so if spirits were still hanging around, I wondered how he could know. Could he see them? Feel them? Or was he just playing with my mind again? He was supposed to be teaching music anyway, so I didn't ask.

I counted thirteen different sized mounds surrounding one big mound situated in the middle. The big one was said to be at least twenty feet high. They were spread across a broad open field, and from our vantage point, they looked as if they were but small bumps on the land. It was hard to believe that they were really that large.

"Those are notes, big notes," Michael said, nodding across the river to the mounds.

"What do you mean?" I asked.

"Signs left by the native people. Those mounds are like big notes, but you have to be far away from them in order to read them as a group. Tom Brown Jr. is a tracker, so he would call them tracks. I am a musician, so I call them notes. If a good tracker can tell a lot about the people who left those tracks, a good musician should be able to do the same."

After a few minutes of musical mound contemplation, Michael broke the silence.

"Reading tracks is like reading Music, just as making tracks is like making Music. There is no way to move across the landscape without leaving tracks. It matters not whether it is a natural landscape or a musical one. Every time you move, and every time you play a note, a piece of yourself is left behind. There is no way to avoid that.

"Now, the tracker," he explained, continuing to gaze upon the field, "if he is a good one, can see right into the soul of whoever left the tracks. The tracker can tell what the creator of the tracks was thinking, feeling, doing, and more. A good musician should be able to do the same. To learn how to do that takes time, dedication, and intuition, but since you can read Music already, it should come to you easily."

I'd heard of reading palms, tea leaves, hair follicles, and eyes, and Brown's book even talked about reading tracks, but never before had I heard of reading music, at least not in this way.

"Take a good look at these mounds," Michael instructed, waving his hand across the horizon. "Seeing them as a whole is a lot like looking at a piece of Music. A good reader can get an idea of what a piece of Music sounds like just by looking at the whole chart. Now, to get more detail from the Music, we need to move closer. Let's go!"

Without hesitation, he took off running down the hill. He bounced down the small mountain like a deer, and I tried my best to keep up. By the time I made it to the bottom, Michael was already crossing the river and heading over to the mounds. When I finally caught up with him, he was standing on top of the large mound which, I now noticed, was flattened on the top forming a small plateau. From this vantage point, we could clearly see how the smaller mounds were situated in a horseshoe shape around the largest mound.

"The key," Michael stated.

"What?"

"The key, you found it. You are standing on it. Can you see how this mound is like the key center of a piece of Music? Everything else is here to support this larger mound."

"I see," I replied, struggling to understand. "Let me try. The large mound we are standing on is like the key of the song. All the other mounds are here to help define what that key is. This large mound had to be established first before the other mounds, or, let me say the other notes, could be placed. It's clear, standing here in the center, that the smaller mounds are here to help support this larger one. So relating these mounds to music, I can see that the first thing to do is establish a key. How was that?"

"Very good," he answered. "But like I mentioned before, the first thing might not be the key."

"Right, the groove, but in this situation, we're talking about mounds. Wait a minute! Are you saying that the Natives first established a groove before building the mounds?"

"Yes!"

"How so?" I imagined native people dancing to the music while building the mounds. I knew that wasn't what he was talking about, but I couldn't make the connection, at least not yet.

"What did they think about before placing the mounds here?" he asked.

I tried to come up with an answer, but the pure act of trying seemed to push it away.

"I don't know."

"You search for answers the way you search for notes. Let go of the need to be in charge," Michael instructed.

I didn't quite grasp what he was talking about, but I did try to relax. It didn't help. I still couldn't find the answer.

"Can you give me a hint?" I asked.

"Tomorrow we will build an exact replica of this mound in your back yard. Okay?"

"Why?" I asked, not following his logic.

"Finally! I thought you would never get the answer."

"What are you talking about?" I was really confused.

"You don't even get the answers when they come to you. Maybe you are more pitiful than I thought." Michael lowered his head. I could tell he was trying to conceal his laughter by the way his head bounced.

I threw my hands up in frustration. "I still don't get it."

"Why!" Michael blurted.

Feeling more than frustrated, I had to keep myself from shouting. "I don't know why."

"No, listen; they needed a *why*, a reason before they placed the mounds. They didn't just decide to place the mounds in this specific area one day. They had a reason for doing it. Then they decided *where* to place them. Where to place the mounds is the key. Why to place them in the first place is the groove."

"Okay, now I get it." I breathed a heavy sigh of relief. "That should've been easy. Of course they had a reason to place the mounds here. They needed the reason 'why' before they decided 'where' to place 'em, and not the other way around. I understand that clearly now."

"Yes, and now you can see how purpose was their 'groove,' right?" he asked.

"Yes, I can. So, what was their purpose for placing the mounds here?" I asked.

"Let's look closer and see what ideas come to us."

He reached in his waist pack and pulled out a handful of Popsicle sticks. I had no idea what they were for. He started walking around the large mound poking the sticks into the ground. By the time he was finished, there were rows of sticks going up and down the mound in all directions.

"Look here. What do you see?" He was pointing at the ground.

"Grass," I answered, only half joking.

He got down on his knees and motioned for me to do the same. Placing his hands in the grass, he parted the blades carefully. "Think Tom Brown," he suggested.

I answered immediately. "A track, I see it."

"Yes, deer tracks on top of the mounds out here in the open," he replied as he stood up. "Each one of these rows of sticks marks the trail of a different animal coming to the top of this mound."

"I see the sticks, but I'm having trouble seeing the tracks," I admitted.

"If you were in a room and tuned your mind to the color blue, every blue thing in the room would jump out at you. All you have to do here is tune your mind to the appearance of the track I just showed you. Then, like the color blue, the rest of the tracks will appear."

I knew what he was talking about. I'd done it with colors many times before. I could cause myself to recognize any color in a room just by thinking of that color. As soon as I would focus my mind, everything in the room that was even close to the same color I was thinking of would stand out. By focusing on a different color, I could cause that color to stand out. I decided to try it with the track.

I looked down and focused on the deer track at our feet. It was a shade darker than the rest of the grass. I unfocused my eyes and looked around the mound using my peripheral vision. To my surprise, I could see rows of little dark circles all over the mound.

"I see 'em!" I exclaimed.

"Of course you do. There are animal tracks all over these mounds. Tell me this. Why do you think these animals are risking their safety to come here? There is no food or water here, and on top of the mound, they are out in the open where they do not like to be. What draws them to this location?"

"Maybe there's something here for the animals that we don't see," I answered.

"Precisely!" Michael responded with excitement. "And maybe there was something here for the native people too. And maybe there's something here for us, but we just can't see it. What we can't see, but know is there, is usually called what?" he asked.

"Spirit," I answered.

"Exactly! Spirit, the sensed, but unseen. Music is the same. Can you see Music? No? Then what is it really, I ask you?"

I'd heard of the idea of music being spiritual, but he put it in a way that made sense to me.

All of a sudden, without waiting for me to answer his last question, Michael ripped off his boots and took off down the hill running on all fours like an animal. It was a hilarious sight. He bounced up and down, back and forth. Turning and darting like he'd lost his mind, he scampered all over the mound. I'd seen squirrels act like that but never a human.

I could see the enjoyment on his face. His eyes beamed like a young pup's, seeing his first snow. It looked like fun to me too, but I didn't have the courage to join him. After removing the Popsicle sticks from one of the rows, he laid them down beside each track, then motioned for me to join him near the bottom of the hill. Of course, I walked.

"Look," he said. "Musical manuscript."

"What do you mean?" I asked.

"If you allow the track to become the note and the stick to become the stem, each track will look like a musical note. You can then read the animal's gait pattern like a piece of Music."

"Cool!"

"Also," Michael added, "noticing how the animal's feet 'attacked' the ground will tell you even more about the animal. Usually, the sharper the attack of each foot, the shorter the length of time it spends on the ground. This is a lot like Music."

I'd learned from the tracking book that gaits were how you could tell whether the animal was moving fast or slow and that looking at the edges of the track could tell you about the animal's direction and intention. After Michael showed me how to read each group of deer tracks like a measure of music, I could do just that. I could tell instantly that the deer was galloping if the tracks sharply hit the ground in groups of four. Tracks in groups of two meant that the deer was moving more slowly.

It came to me suddenly that the same is true in music. Four notes in a measure versus two notes in a measure lets you know how quickly the notes are moving, even at a glance. The fact that the deer ran across the field but walked on top of the open mound let me know that they were comfortable there.

Paying attention to how the distinct edges of deer hoofs hit the ground enabled me to tell in advance when the animal was going to change directions. I had no idea how Michael could predict those direction changes before he showed me what to look for. Now that I could do it, I felt like Sherlock Holmes.

He showed me how to tell which way an animal was looking, based on how its feet hit the ground. He also told me that if we looked deeper into the tracks, we could look deeper into the track maker. Michael believed that many internal things could be discerned about an animal or a human by studying his tracks. I didn't know what he meant by 'internal,' but what he'd already shown me was enough. Being able to tell so much, just by looking at the ground, seemed magical to me. I could only imagine what it must be like having the ability to do the same thing by listening to someone's music.

A sad person often plays music in a minor key, while a major key might suggest a happy mood. That, I already knew. I could even tell when a person was extremely nervous just by listening to his music. Maybe, like tracks, music *is* a doorway allowing one to peek into a person's spirit. The thought of that was really intriguing. I was excited to learn more.

"This is a spiritual place," Michael spoke, after we galloped our way back to the top of the hill. "The natives know it. The animals know it, and now, you know it."

"But what's your proof? How do you know that this is a spiritual place, more than any other place?" I inquired.

"Proof? What is proof but someone's perspective? And tell me, what importance does proof have anyway? Did you learn from the experience? Now, *that* is important!"

"But what makes it more spiritual than any other place?" I asked.

"I didn't say that this place was *more* spiritual than any other place," he continued. "I said that it is *a* spiritual place and the natives know it. Think about this. You looked at this place from high atop Mace Bluff and you saw beauty. You then came and stood atop the largest mound and you saw beauty. And now, you look into the mound at the tracks of the animals that walk across her face, and still, you see beauty. Now close your eyes and tell me what you see."

I did as he asked and again saw beauty.

"Good. From four different perspectives you have viewed this wonderful place, and each view has generated the same feeling—beauty! How can you be wrong?

"Beauty is something you experience, not something you prove. Can you tell me what beauty is, or can you only give me your perspective on it? Can science define beauty? Can you see or touch it, or can you just see and touch something that possesses its quality? Beauty is invisible, individual, and intangible. Interesting, isn't it? It is something you know, yet technically, it is not there. How can this be? Like Music, it lives inside you, and you impress its qualities on whatever you choose.

"People have spoken about beauty for centuries. A wise man in the 1800s once said: 'The beautiful is that in which the many, still seen as many, become one.' There is truth in that statement, but in simpler terms it could be stated as another wise man did. He wrote, 'Beauty is truth, truth beauty.' That is easily understandable."

Standing up straight, he spread his arms wide and closed his eyes.

"The Natives knew and still know that this is a spiritual place because they choose it to be, and you have chosen the same. And nestled here in the bend of the beautiful Harpeth River you can see why."

He quickly opened his eyes and leaned forward asking me one last question.

"If this place is beautiful, and 'beauty' is invisible, then what is this place?"

"A spiritual place!" I exclaimed.

"Thank you! Now we can go."

Technique

Are you using magic?
Yes, I am. It's called technique.

I was speechless. I stood there for a moment letting his words linger in my mind. A breeze blew across my face as he turned and walked away. It chilled my skin. Somehow, I felt, his words were connected to the breeze. I can't explain it, but it was as if his message was carried through the air and into my ears by the wind. And like the wind, it hit before I could see it coming.

After retrieving our Popsicle sticks, we didn't speak another word all the way back to the car. When we arrived, Michael broke the silence.

"Watch," he said.

I hadn't noticed, but he had picked up two small pieces of wood. One was a straight, thin, round stick about fourteen inches long. The other was a short flat board, a little thicker than the stick. He knelt down on one knee, placing the flat board on the ground. Holding the board down with his foot, he held the longer stick between his palms, perpendicular to the flat board (forming an upside-down T).

By rapidly rubbing his palms together, he rolled the thin stick back and forth. With his body leaning over his hands, providing downward pressure, he caused the stick to rub and spin back and forth against the board creating friction and heat. Within a few seconds, the wood started smoking. A few seconds later, he stopped rolling the stick.

"Look," he said.

I looked down, and there was a red hot coal lying beside the flat board. After allowing me a good look, he transferred the coal onto a pile of dry grasses. Then he gently picked up the pile and blew on it three times. During his third breath, the whole thing burst into flames right in his hands. It was both amazing and beautiful to watch.

Michael told me that what he'd used was called a hand-drill. I'd seen someone make a fire using that technique once before on a television show, but I'd never seen anything quite like what Michael demonstrated. The whole process took less than one minute, and if he hadn't stopped to let me watch, it would've probably taken less than thirty seconds. (A year or so later, I practiced making fire using the hand-drill and bow-drill techniques. It was not easy to do. To make a fire in that short amount of time still seems nearly impossible.)

After holding the flaming bundle for a few seconds, Michael tossed it on the ground and looked at me.

"Your turn," he suggested as he stamped out the flames.

"Okay, I'll give it a try."

I knelt down and did my best to repeat what I'd just seen, practically mangling the two pieces of wood in the process. The stick in my hands kept wobbling back and forth, slipping off the flat board on the ground. After about two minutes of struggling, I was exhausted. I dropped the stick and sat back, tired and sweaty.

Michael chuckled, picked up the stick, and had the wood smoking again within a few seconds.

"How'd you do that?" I asked, still out of breath. "Are you using magic?" I was only half joking.

"Yes, I am. It's called *technique*," he answered. "Without proper technique, nothing can happen."

"Can you teach me the proper technique for making a fire?" I asked, forgetting one of his first rules.

"No, I can't," he answered with his familiar sly grin.

"Why not?" I asked. "Oh, right. Will you *show* me the proper technique, please?" I was slowly adapting to his style of teaching.

"I would be delighted."

We knelt down and he showed me how and where to place my hands and feet. He told me that the reason the stick, made of horseweed, was wobbling against the cedar board was that I was favoring my stronger hand.

"Use both hands equally," he instructed. "Most musicians favor their stronger hand. They may never realize it, but if the problem is not corrected, it will surely hinder their progress. And here," he said pointing at the sticks, "if the problem is not corrected, you will never make a fire."

After a few more starts and stops, corrections and adjustments, I had smoke. It wasn't much, but it was smoke. Michael laughed and told me that I was sweating so much while attempting to start a fire, I would likely put out my coal before I could ever ignite a flame. I fell back on the ground, spent and breathing hard. Michael spoke so that I didn't have to.

"To play Music, good technique is a must. You can know all the notes in the world. You can have the best ideas in the world, but you need good technique to get them out. Your technique can even be unorthodox, but if it is inadequate, you will not be able to express yourself freely; you will frustrate yourself instead. Good technique allows you to use all the other elements of Music at will."

He knelt down and proceeded to make another coal as easily as he'd made the first. He never stopped talking during the process. I relaxed on the ground, watching and listening.

"Your technique should be at such a high level that you can forget about it. Eventually, you will even forget about your bass. Only then can you remember how to play Music. Think about talking. When you talk, the words are your notes. Your tongue, diaphragm, mouth, teeth, lips, and so on are your instruments. How you use them to push air across your vocal cords and through your lips to form words is your technique, but you rarely think about that."

His coal was still smoking, so I threw some grass on top of it. The grass was moist, which almost put out the coal, but

Michael came to the rescue. Blowing on it with a couple short breaths, he had it smoking again within seconds.

"When you were a baby," he continued, "your technique was not adequate enough to allow you to speak like everyone else. You would babble on and on trying to work it out and be understood. Not having the proper control of your instrument caused you to cry."

He frowned comically as if he was an upset child. I had to laugh.

"After many months, you finally developed the control allowing you to say the things you wanted to say. That made you happy. The feeling of joy encouraged you to learn more."

He stood up smiling, raising his hands into the air.

"Notice you did not develop your speaking technique through diligent practice, at least not the type of practice you are familiar with. Your parents didn't lock you in a room and make you work on it three hours a day, and they didn't make you take lessons. You learned to speak through a natural process. Musicians could benefit from looking at this process.

"When learning Music, we think we need to concentrate really hard on something until we achieve success. We also think we should lock ourselves in what we call the 'woodshed' for at least a few hours each day and focus on what we are doing. We practice our scales, modes, and techniques over and over until they become second nature. This, we think, is the only way of attaining the level of master musician. I propose a different path."

He bent down over the coal and waved his hand one time, creating a breeze. As he stood back up, the grass burst into flames. My eyes widened. He didn't react.

"Do you have to concentrate to speak English?" he inquired. "When you are playing Music at your best, are you concentrating? Do you want to have to concentrate every time you do anything well? No, you don't."

I was tense, but he seemed at ease. Concentrating hard, I tried to keep up with what he was both doing and saying. Between listening to his words and watching him manipulate the fire, I was getting left behind. He began to speak again, so I did my best to pay attention.

"If a policeman walked up to you right now and commanded you to walk a straight line, you would probably have a hard time doing it. Why?" He stood up and acted as if he were walking on a tightrope. "Because you would start concentrating on doing it 'right.'"

He fell to the ground as if losing his balance. Looking up at me he continued. "You don't have to concentrate to walk. So when you start *trying* to concentrate, your body does not like it and you lose your balance. If you were to do that in front of the policeman, you could end up in jail, and that is exactly what happens to most of us when we try to play Music. We allow ourselves to be trapped in the jails of our own minds." He clenched his fists in front of him pantomiming being behind bars.

"There is a time for concentrating and a time for not concentrating," he said. "Concentration is similar to focusing the rays of the sun into one point by use of a magnifying glass.

Amazing amounts of heat can be produced by using this method. You used to do it as a kid. Am I right?"

I smiled but didn't answer. Of course he was right. I thought about the few times I'd played with fire as a kid. I'd always enjoyed starting fires with a magnifying glass. There was something about focusing the sun's rays down to one point that intrigued me. I thought about the possibilities of doing it with one's mind. Michael sat down in a full lotus position before continuing, interrupting my childhood recollections.

"Concentrating or focusing is great for projecting your thoughts or your will. This usually means closing down the mind in a way that shuts out all other factors, except for the one thing you are attempting to achieve."

Resting his hands on his knees, he turned his palms upward touching his thumbs and middle fingers together. Closing his eyes, he continued speaking.

"Miracles can be produced through concentration of this type, but it takes control. If the proper method or technique is used, the mind can produce much more heat than the largest magnifying glass, but depending on the situation, that may not be the most productive use of the mind.

"When it is time to receive information, *opening* the mind works best." He opened his eyes to stress his point. "It is like taking the power of your mind and opening it up to whatever information is out there. The mind cannot achieve its true potential until you have mastered each of these techniques. Like yin and yang, they work together to complete the whole. If you do not want to have to concentrate every time you play your bass, you should not have to concentrate every time you practice."

I should've realized that myself. I hated having to concentrate just to make music. I knew that whenever I was performing at my best, I wasn't concentrating at all; I was in the "zone." Still frustrated at how much I was having to concentrate at that moment, I kept quiet and listened.

"Kids know how to do it instinctively, but most adults unintentionally do their best to rob them of this beautiful quality. Children learn faster than most adults ever will, because their minds are open. They may not realize what they're doing, but by opening their minds to all the information available to them, their power of imagination and creation becomes limitless, which means their potential is limitless. You don't get an imagination like that through concentration."

Michael was usually like a kid himself, never sitting still for long. Though he used his arms to gesture, this was as long as I'd seen him sit in one position. Still sitting in lotus position, he removed his hat and used it to fan the coal that was still smoldering next to him. It appeared as if he was sending smoke signals. Now, using his hat to gesture, he continued speaking.

"Like this smoke, knowledge is in the air. All the knowledge that ever existed, or ever will exist, is here already: right here, right now. If you can tune in to the correct frequency you can pick up any information you want. We think the brain creates knowledge, but I am here to tell you that the brain creates nothing. The brain receives, or more accurately, it discovers. It would be a miracle in and of itself to think that everything in this world came from the brain, a jelly-like mass the size of a grapefruit. The brain can receive information and then use it. But create it? No!" He lowered his head, shaking it back and forth.

Then he quickly waved his finger through the smoke, and it swirled, slithering around like a snake. The smoke slowly danced its way toward me. I leaned back, imagining a forked tongue tasting the air and testing my comfort level.

Once the snake dissipated, he placed his safari hat on the ground completely covering the coal. It caused his hat to start smoldering. I was confused by his actions once again. Enjoying my confused look, he smiled and continued talking.

"Music comes out of a radio, but is Music inside the box? No! Music is in the air. The radio has the ability to tune in to the proper frequency and pick up whatever Music it wants, but it does not create it.

"Imagine if the radio could open up and play all Music at once. The result would be chaos. Unless it's 'tuned in' to what we want it to receive, it's not really working at all. Many people lose control in Life by doing exactly that. They open up to the 'All,' without the proper control necessary to assimilate all the information. The result, unless prepared, is chaos. Remember, all knowledge is in the air, and since you breathe in this air, all knowledge is also in you. The radio demonstrates what I am talking about perfectly."

As he finished his monologue, he placed the still smoking hat back onto his head making it appear as if his head was on fire. From his cross-legged position, he smiled proudly. Again, I found myself marveling at just how childlike the strange man's actions could appear. I got the feeling that he was using the radio technique right then to receive the information that he was feeding me. He seemed too crazy to come up with it on his own.

I could use this skill. It surely would be nice not having to keep all of my knowledge in my brain at all times. I thought I could feel my head smoke as well.

All of a sudden, I realized something about my own method of learning. I usually tried to block out all other things so I could cram new information into my head. It rarely worked. My brain, being cramped already, would usually spit the information back out. I could imagine a "No Vacancy" sign posted on the door of my brain. *No more information please.*

As if reading my thoughts, Michael asked, "How does this pertain to technique?"

"I think I know," I answered.

Michael placed his hat on my head. It was still smoking.

"Now," he instructed, "don't think; either you know or you don't. Tell me what you know."

"Okay, when I play at my best, I'm not thinking. I'm in the 'zone.' Music is flowing through me, but this flow is broken sometimes when I make a mistake. My mistakes are often caused by frustration, and making mistakes often causes me to become frustrated. Many times, poor technique is at the root of the problem. Poor technique robs me of free expression. It's like I hear what I wanna play, but my technique doesn't allow it to come out.

"Now," I continued, "in order for me to play freely, I need good technique, but I don't wanna be thinking about my technique while I'm playing any more than I wanna be thinking about my mouth when I'm talking. So, when I practice, I use 'concentration' to learn what the technique is. Then I use 'not concentrating' to get completely comfortable using the technique. Combining the two concentration methods allows me to get a complete grasp of the technique."

I surprised myself. Somehow, I was finally getting it. I didn't know where the information was coming from, but I was open to it and it was flowing through me. I wasn't ready to stop. Feeling the energy, I kept talking.

"If 'not concentrating' is where I want to end up, I need to add it to my practice routine. Combining 'concentrating' with 'not concentrating' is necessary to complete the circle. This, like you said, is yin and yang. Both parts are needed to complete the whole. We know how to concentrate and we know how to practice concentrating, but do we know how to practice 'not concentrating'? I need to figure that out for the circle to be complete."

"What can you use to practice 'not concentrating'?" Michael asked as he removed the still smoldering hat from my head.

"Television," I replied. That was an easy one for me.

"Do you think that television can be of any assistance?"

"Of course, it can," I responded. "If I practice my techniques while watching a television show it might allow another part of my brain to be activated. This would simulate 'not concentrating' while playing music."

"I thought television was a negative thing," Michael said, raising both eyebrows.

"Well, then, that's what you thought," I answered with

complete authority. I didn't know where my newly found authority was coming from, but I had it and was running with it. I sat down trying to form my own lotus position. My legs screamed, "No!" Hearing Michael chuckle under his breath, I scrapped the lotus idea and decided to display my authority with words instead.

"Television is only negative or positive depending on how you use it," I continued. "Like a Zen master once said: 'Nothing is either good or bad until,' uh . . . 'we think it is,' or, no, 'until thinking it's so,' or something like that." It was my turn to be poetic, and I blew it. "Anyway, if we're gonna watch it, why not use it to our advantage? That's not the only way. Day-dreaming, night-dreaming, sitting in nature, meditation, and many other things could help me learn how to 'not concentrate' so that we can spend more time feeling the music. If we had to concentrate all the time on the techniques and the instruments we use to talk, we would never be able to say anything worthwhile. Being able to concentrate, or not, is necessary before one can reach his full potential. If television can help me with it, that's what I'll use. You may choose to use something else if you want to." I folded my arms (instead of my legs) and nodded my head one time.

"Spoken with true understanding," Michael commented as he bowed down to my feet. "Teach me! Will you teach me, master?"

"No! I can teach you nothing," I responded, patting him on the head.

We laughed for a long time about my narration. Michael seemed pleased with it. I was shocked about what I'd said and the authority I'd expressed because I didn't know where it had come from. I knew what I'd said was accurate, though, and I was sure of myself like never before.

Without warning, Michael hopped up, picked up three sticks, and started juggling them. I was impressed. What he did next was even more surprising. He walked to the front of the car and used the sticks to play a rhythmic pattern on the hood—and never stopping juggling the whole time.

"That's pretty good," I remarked.

"How's my drumming?" he asked.

"Great!"

"Close your eyes and listen."

I closed my eyes and listened closely. In doing so, I realized that his drumming was not that good at all. His juggling was great, but his rhythm was unsteady, mediocre at best.

"Fooled you with my performance," Michael stated as he caught the sticks in one hand.

"I guess you did."

"A great performance can make anyone sound good."

"I see."

"Technique often serves the same purpose," he added. "The use of flashy techniques can cause the audience to start watching and stop listening. At the appropriate time, this can be a useful tool. The problem with it is, more times than not, it is the musician who stops listening and not the audience. That should never happen. More and more bass players are learning the flashy techniques first." For some reason, he pointed at me as he spoke. "They should develop a more solid foundation before they venture off in that direction. It doesn't matter what the technique is; just make it solid before you make it flashy."

I knew that he was talking about me, so I fired back with my own comment. "I've seen you use flashy techniques before."

"Yes you have, but when you close your eyes, what do you hear? You still hear good Music. You don't have to watch it to enjoy it. I make sure that even my flashiest techniques are used musically. I can't say that about all players."

I could've tried, but there was really nothing for me to say. Still feeling a bit defensive, I kept quiet and listened.

"Here's the difference," he continued. "My techniques are not born out of the need to be flashy. They are born out of the desire to produce with my hands what I hear with my mind. Usually, if I keep my mind focused on Music, the technique will create itself. Remember, like talking, techniques are tools and not the end result."

I nodded in agreement trying not to let my insecurity show. Michael didn't seem concerned; he just kept on talking.

"Many musicians get caught up, way too caught up, in the technique when it could benefit them to get caught up in the Music. Some of them measure their accomplishments based on whether they've mastered certain techniques or not. That, to me, is like being proud of yourself because you can curl your tongue in two or three loops. That's all good and well, and maybe you should be proud; I am not here to say one way or another, but if it is Music we are talking about, maybe these musicians should reprioritize."

I opened my mouth to speak, but he held up a finger.

I sat on the hood of the car, swallowed my words, and listened.

"To the real musician, techniques are nothing more than tools to get you somewhere. We only need to focus on them long enough to find the correct and most efficient ways of doing things. Once we do that, our attention turns back to Music. The more we feel Music, the faster the technique falls into place. I know musicians who have worked on simple techniques for years with little progress." He shook his head. "That is because for years their attention has been on technique, not Music. That is a mistake."

"I haven't heard you call anything a mistake before now," I remarked.

"I only call it that in relation to what you want your outcome to be. If your goal is to speak Music right now, concentrating on a technique for years may be viewed as a mistake, a waste of valuable time and effort."

I tried to convince myself that he was talking *to* me and not *about* me. It was hard. I'd been working on some techniques for a long time to no avail; it was frustrating to say the least. If Michael could help me with this problem, I was ready to give in to him once again.

"I wanna learn to use my thumb like a pick the way you do," I said, moving my hand up and down. "I've been working on this double thumb technique for too long now."

"You think of double thumbing as a new technique, so it makes it hard for you," he explained. "If you think of it as an old technique that guitarists have used for decades, it will be easy. You are being trapped by your mind."

He pantomimed holding the bars of a jail cell again. He shook the bars, reminding me of his earlier comment.

"The first thing you must tell yourself is that you can already do the technique," he continued. "Once you do that, you will be two giant steps ahead even before you start. The final step will be convincing your hands that they also know what to do." He looked at his hands as if he was talking to them. Then he looked up at me and asked a question.

"If you were to practice this technique twenty hours a day for one solid week, do you think that you would then be able to do it?"

"Of course I would."

"Then why spend years learning something that you know you could learn in a week?"

"I . . . uh . . . well . . . if I . . . hmm . . ." I didn't have an answer, so Michael continued speaking.

"At the end of that week, what would have changed about you? Would your thumb, hand, or arm muscles be bigger? Would the skin on your hands be thicker? What would be different about you, one week later, that would allow you to do what you couldn't do before?"

"Well—" I thought for a moment before answering. "I don't think my muscles would change much in that short amount of time. They might be sore but not bigger. I think the main difference would be coordination. Yeah, I would feel better coordinated at the end of the week."

"Okay, coordination," he mumbled. "What is coordination?"

He looked at me as if he was confused, which confused

me. I rested my head in my hands trying to think. It was the first time I'd ever been asked that question. I sat there silent, unable to answer.

"What is coordination but a form of convincing?" he asked, spreading his hands and hunching his shoulders.

"What?"

"Is coordination anything more than a form of convincing?" he asked again.

"What do you mean?"

"Through practice and repetition, could it be that you are just convincing your muscles and your mind that they already know what to do? Maybe that's the primary function of practicing."

"Uh, maybe so," I replied, trying to keep up.

He pointed his long index finger at me and continued. "Now, what do you think would happen if you could convince yourself first, at the beginning of your quest? In other words, before you start practicing anything, convince yourself you can already do it. What would happen then? I'll tell you. Depending on how well you do at the convincing part, you will cut your practice time in half. Use the full potential of your mind, and practice will become a thing of the past. How do you think I can play any instrument I choose? Do you think I've practiced them all? Can you imagine a master like the Buddha having to practice before he could play the bass?"

He stuck out his stomach and played an air-bass. It was a funny sight, but there was no time for his levity. I had to put my vision of the bass-playing Buddha aside. There was more learning to be done.

"That idea sounds interesting to me. It even makes sense, but that's make-believe, right? It's not truth. I can't imagine actually doing it. I mean, can I really convince myself enough so that I don't have to practice?"

"Can you?" he replied in his familiar fashion.

"Stop it!" I responded in my own familiar way. "Just tell me the truth."

"Truth? What is truth? Truth is up to you. You make your truth; no one else does. Tell yourself that it takes a long time to learn something, and it probably will. Convincingly put yourself at the end of the path and you will find yourself looking back at the beginning. It is all up to you."

He seemed convinced. I wasn't. He pointed his finger at me and continued speaking.

"But know this: you cannot fool yourself. You cannot half-heartedly tell yourself that you can do something and then expect to be able to do it. You must be honest. From all levels of your being, you must know what you are talking about. If you want to practice anything, practice knowing that you can do whatever you set your complete mind to. Don't practice believing; practice knowing!"

"Okay then, how am I supposed to do that?"

"How are you supposed to do that?" Michael raised an eyebrow and paused.

I hated it when he answered my questions with my own questions, and he knew it. I think he took pride in being able to frustrate me so easily. Knowing I wouldn't answer, he continued—continued frustrating me, that is.

"There are a million and two different ways to do it. Which one are you looking for?" he asked.

Out of frustration, I gave a sarcastic reply. "I only want the *eight hundred and forty second one.*"

"Oh, that one. I don't know if you're ready for that one." He lowered his head as if he was really thinking about it. I could see him smiling. That bothered me.

"Stop jerking me around," I shouted, losing my cool and banging my fist on the hood of the car. "You feed me this nonsense about how I can learn to quit practicing, and then you leave me hanging. Teach me something I can use."

Michael spoke in an offbeat tone. "Hmm, the need to practice, when you are ready, you will lose, not before, and not after."

"What is that supposed to mean?"

"I don't know. It just sounded good, like something Yoda would say, so I figured I would try it out. I like Yoda, don't you? I remember seeing *Star Wars* for the first time when I—"

This time, I interrupted him, raising my hand and putting my open palm in his face.

"Come on now, enough! Stop messing with me and get back to the point. Tell me how I can learn faster. I don't need to completely get rid of practice. I just want to learn faster. Can you give me a concrete tool that I can use to do that, or not?"

He recognized my sternness but was not ready to stop joking with me.

"Okay, okay, calm down," he responded. "I see, you just want to sit on the sidelines while I score all the touchdowns for you. Isn't it more fun to be *in* the game?"

"Michael!" I shouted. "Enough!" I hopped off the hood of the car and acted like I was going to walk away. I wasn't convincing and I knew it, so I turned back around and stomped my foot like a child which made him laugh. This irritated me even more. "Stop playing and help me out!" I pleaded.

"Okay," he conceded, still smiling. "I'll be serious, but just for a little while."

"Thank you." I was feeling a little victorious.

"Ask yourself a question enough times and the answer will appear," Michael replied. "And since you are a nice guy, I will give you some help."

"It's about time!" I groaned.

Michael took a step closer and placed a hand on my shoulder. Looking me in the eyes, he spoke. "We know that good techniques are a must, but most of us don't have good techniques for learning them. I have already given you most of what you need to know." He nodded, turned and pretended to walk away. He was more convincing than I was. I panicked.

"Wait a minute! Stop! You have? What do you mean?" I asked, trying to cut through my frustration so I could remember what had been said.

He sat down on the ground and proceeded to put his boots back on.

"Remember," he said, "start by knowing you can already do the technique. Believing it won't do; you must know it with all your being. Using 'concentration' to focus and project your thoughts is very valuable, as well as learning to use 'not concentrating.' This will open your mind to all that is available to you. You must know how and when to use both of these tools to achieve the greatest accomplishments. You understand that now, don't you?"

"No," I answered, still a bit puzzled.

Without tying his laces, he stood up and took a step closer to me. When he spoke, he spoke slowly, displaying the patience of a saint. "If I have a musical passage that I want to play, but don't yet possess the required technique, I will focus on that technique just long enough to understand the exact movements required to do it in the most efficient way. After that, which usually doesn't take very long, I pull my attention back inside my mind to where Music is. In other words, I release the technique. I let it go. I detach from it. Once that is done, the technique usually develops rapidly on its own. If it doesn't, I will give the technique a little more attention. The key is this: I never lose sight of my real agenda, which is to make Music. This is the same method I use for talking. Rarely do I ever think about talking technique; I just talk."

"Finally, something I understand," I stated with relief, letting him know that most of what he had said was confusing.

"Here, try this," he offered. "The next time you set your mind on learning something, act as if you can already do it. Ask yourself, 'What would it sound like if I could already do this technique?' Then, do it! If done honestly, you may not have to start from the beginning of the learning cycle. You may be able to skip a few steps."

"Is it okay to skip steps?" I asked. "Won't I risk missing something?"

"Skipping steps may not always be as thorough, but the better you learn to use your mind, the more knowledge you will bring with you no matter how many steps are skipped. As long as you are always listening, you should have no problems."

He moved a step closer, his nose almost touching mine. The energy coming from his brown eyes alerted me to the importance of what he was about to say. Spoken in almost a whisper, his words gave me a chill.

"Whether we are talking about Music or Life, good technique is important. Understand that just learning techniques is not enough. You must make a choice, a conscious choice to take one road or another. Good or bad, each is narrow, making it difficult for U-turns.

"Know that the mind is a powerful tool, and that its power can respond to you both positively or negatively. Learning to use it completely should not be taken lightly. This is where technique as well as intention and attention come into play. Many people have gotten sucked into the black hole of the mind, never to return again."

With that comment, he got into the car and closed the door. Pointing out the window, he offered final instructions.

"Don't forget to put out the fire, the one on the ground *and* the one in your head."

I looked back at the grass. It was ablaze from the coal.

"That will be the easy one to put out," I thought out loud. I heard him chuckle from inside the car.

As I danced around stomping out the flames, I thought about what he'd told me. I didn't know why, but it sounded as if the teacher was giving his student a warning.

But a warning of what?

Emotion/Feel

A child playing air-guitar
plays no wrong notes.

The sweet smell of burnt cedar filled the car. The aroma, like incense, calmed my nerves and freed my mind, leaving it receptive to the teaching taking place in this portable meditation room made of wheels and steel. I do some of my best thinking while driving. Though we hadn't said a word since the car started moving, I was still absorbing all that he'd previously talked about. Since we had about twenty miles left to go, I was ready for more. Feeling in the mood, I asked again about the elements of music.

"We have decided on ten that we will explore," Michael replied, "and we have looked at three of them already. Let's review them, shall we? We have explored all twelve *notes*. You shouldn't be afraid of them anymore. Through bluegrass

Music and tracking, you were able to find the worlds that live inside each note. This could be put into the category called *articulation*. From making fire, we touched on the topic of *technique*. What element of Music would you like to look at next?"

I had an idea already. "On top of the mound you talked about feeling beauty. We said that feel would be one of our elements, and I relate feeling to emotion. How would emotion fit into our list? Can you talk about that?"

"*Emotion* is a powerful force," Michael stated. "*E*, meaning 'energy,' and *motion*, meaning 'activity.' So, *emotion* can be looked at as 'energy in motion' or 'active energy.' If you play with the vowels, hidden meanings can be brought out of many words. Looked at another way, *motion* or *mu-tone*, means 'the mother of all vibration.' Now you can see the power in this word. Emotion is a key element in Music and in Life."

Michael was again speaking in strange terms. I knew that he wouldn't leave me behind for long, so I listened, waiting for him to say something I could understand.

"Emotion, properly directed, can cause anything to happen. A mediocre musician can win over an audience by sheer emotion alone. Remember, any one of the ten elements, raised to a very high level, can be used in a way that overshadows the fact that the musician is lacking in skill of the other nine.

"A child playing air-guitar knows no technique or Music theory and probably doesn't even own a real guitar, yet plays no wrong notes. The sheer enjoyment he exudes overshadows any of his shortcomings. This is emotion in action.

"Blues musicians display a similar quality," Michael continued. "They are rarely the best technical players; they are usually self-taught and may only know a few chords, but they have a tremendous amount of soul. Walk into any real blues bar and you instantly feel their emotion. That is what comes across through their Music first. The audience feels the 'realness' of what the musician is putting out.

"Blind musicians are the same. Have you ever noticed that all blind musicians play with a remarkable amount of feel—not some of them, all of them? Also, why is it that when a blind musician becomes popular, he stays that way? Think about it." He closed his eyes, rocking his body back and forth in his seat before continuing. "A famous blind musician will be someone that your parents and your children listen to. Why? I'll tell you. It is because they fill their Music with tremendous amounts of true emotion, and that is what they get across to their listeners."

I'd never thought about that, but I knew what he'd said about blind musicians was true. Whenever I want to think or feel deeply about something, I will often close my eyes. Sometimes, I'll close my eyes to hear better. Food even tastes different with my eyes closed. Using this technique has also allowed me to raise the sensitivity in my hands while feeling for my car keys at the bottom of my bag. I realized that closing my eyes was a tool I frequently used, although unconsciously.

I thought about all the blind musicians I'd ever played with. Michael was right; every one of them played with an incredible amount of feel. None of them were flashy players. Even my blind classmate from high school had played piano with a natural feel. Everyone used to love hearing him play. And now that I thought about it, every blind musician I knew could also sing. I wondered if there was a correlation.

Finally, Michael was making sense. I wanted to close my eyes at that moment so that I could hear him better, but since I was driving, I thought better of it. I just kept my eyes and mind open but my mouth shut while Michael continued talking.

"Now, blues musicians are usually singing about all the negative things that have happened to them. Most listeners can relate to their stories, and because of that, the listener also gets emotional. The listener's emotions get caught up in the emotions of the performer causing the two to mix; thus you get what I call *blending emotions*.

"Blending emotions is what happens when two people fall in love. It is also what a psychic can use to read your thoughts or what a politician often uses to impose his will upon the public. Two or more people blending their positive emotions can cause miraculous things to happen. The opposite is also true. Two or more people blending negative emotions can cause catastrophes from illness to world wars, from crucifixions to shopping malls." Michael kept a straight face, but I couldn't help but laugh.

"Emotion uncontrolled can cause a person to spiral out of control. The cause of this chaotic spiral is often difficult to recognize until it is too late. Most times this lack of control will surface in a musician's Life before it shows up in his Music. Do you know of any musicians who fit into this category?"

"Of course I do." I could think of at least ten musicians who fit the description right off the bat, some of them professionals and some of them personal friends. They were all incredibly gifted players. Many of the famous ones have even changed the way we think about music. But they all seemed to lose control for some reason. You could hear the struggle in some of the musicians' music, but others' music showed no signs. Was it a chemical imbalance, an inherited mental trait, or the result of a drug addiction? Or was it like Michael said? Had they merely lost control of their emotions?

Michael continued, "A politician is not allowed to get too emotional in public, so what he does is drop subtle hints that, over time, cause the public to get emotional. Once the same emotions are generated by enough people, the politician can use it to steer the public in his desired direction. Fear is an emotion that is often used in this way. A smart politician knows that if he can create fear in enough people, those people will give up what they truly want in order to give the politician what he says they need.

"The same is often true with preachers, but they usually take the opposite approach and use a slightly different technique. In order to be considered a good preacher, one must show *a lot* of emotion. It does not matter whether the emotion is genuine or not; it is the amount that matters. He will show so much emotion when he preaches that his congregation gets caught up in it. At some point they're so caught up that they stop paying attention to what the preacher is preaching. That allows some preachers to say nothing at all and still get an 'amen.'

"Have you ever noticed that the church is often the most expensive building in the neighborhood? Why is that? Many people read the Bible. If the preacher is preaching what is already in the Bible, you already know what he is going to say. What makes you want to give him your money? 'Oh, I am giving it to God,' they'll say. Well, what is God going to buy? 'No, I mean, I'm giving it to the church, paying my tithe.' If God is everywhere, shouldn't you be able to pay your tithe everywhere? So, I ask, what is it that causes you to give the church your money? I tell you, whether it is love, fear, or something in between, it is emotion!"

What he said touched a nerve. It resurfaced an old memory of a time when I was singled out in church by the local pastor for not playing his version of gospel music. He made a big deal in front of the whole congregation. I kept quiet. He had piled on so much emotion that I was shocked that he was talking about me. *Whose fault is it that you can't hear the gospel in my music or recognize the gospel in my talent?* I remember thinking. *Where does my talent come from? Where does all talent come from?* I knew the answers back then even though the pastor acted as if he didn't. Many of the church members were friends of mine, but none of them came to my defense.

I sat in church feeling a mix of shame, humility, and betrayal, but for some reason, even though I was very young, I also felt a sense of self-assuredness. I didn't allow the pastor's words to bring me too far down. For him to single me out because of my music let me know that what I was doing was powerful. My mom and dad always told me that church was inside me, not inside a building. I felt good about myself for knowing what I knew. Obviously, I never went back to that church.

I felt more 'in church' spending time with Michael. He'd been talking all along about the power of music. My memory of the pastor connected me to these statements. I wished that church officials could get a dose of Michael's teachings. Public officials could also benefit from spending a day with him. I imagined Michael running for public office. I could see him standing in front of a large crowd delivering his speech: *"Vote for me, or not, and I will promise you nothing!"*

As if he was following along with the story in my mind, Michael allowed my memories to fade before he continued where he'd left off.

"Many people distrust politicians because of their lack of emotion. Many preachers, on the other hand, pile on so much emotion that it causes some people to doubt their authenticity. This causes more distrust. And more times than not, people are correct in both cases.

"Now, listen to what I am about to tell you: Musicians do not have to be believed in. We do not have to be trusted. Our Music speaks for itself without the listener having to know anything about us. Music touches people's emotions in a way that nothing else can. When people find a musician they like, they are usually fans for Life. If they like the musician *and* his Music, they will open up their hearts to whatever that musician has to say. It matters not what country the musician or the fan comes from. Music is a language that all understand. It goes beyond and breaks down barriers. This makes the musician very powerful, and with power comes responsibility."

The thought of becoming more powerful through music was interesting, but when I actually thought about it, I didn't feel that powerful at all. I couldn't even pay my rent. I was ready to make a comment, but Michael wasn't finished.

"We create and release powerful emotions within ourselves and others through a realm called entertainment. The word 'entertainment' can imply that one has 'entered into attainment' or 'atonement' which means 'at-one-ment.' You could also call it *in-tune-ment*. Whatever you call it, just know that it represents a high level. So when you partake as a spectator, you may be watching someone who has attained this level. But you are not only watching; the artist is allowing you to join him at this level. If you join him, it allows both you and the artist to reach even higher levels. As a spectator, you are actually able to push the artist to these higher levels. A gifted artist will carry you with him."

"That sounds cool," I said.

"It can be an extraordinary experience, but you must be careful with whom you blend. An artist who has attained high levels of negativity and puts out those emotions can cause large numbers of people who blend with him to unwittingly create and spread incredible amounts of negative energy. The only time you may want to blend with those types is when you have enough positive energy to dilute his negative energy. You must have a great deal of control over yourself before attempting something like this. Entertainment of this type may still be enjoyable, but you must know who you are dealing with when it comes to blending.

"The cool thing about entertainment is that it is a choice.

It is not like politics, where we are un-American if we do not take part, or like 'good ole' religion, where for thousands of years we've been told what will happen to us if we don't get some. Music is still a choice, free and unencumbered. This is beautiful to some and frightening to others."

It was hard to understand why musical freedom would be frightening to anyone, but I knew that what he said was true. It was this very freedom that caused that pastor to single me out in church. Many times this freedom is threatened and challenged by the political system that makes up the music business. Radio used to be driven by the public. Now it's driven by business. It seems that artists have to 'water down' their music in order to be successful. That causes many great musicians to sacrifice their freedom in order to get their music on the radio. Was it that way in the past? I wondered if fear had caused the change. How and why would anyone fear music?

Once again, as if reading my thoughts, Michael spoke. "Politicians know how powerful musicians and their Music can be. That is why, even to this day, politicians keep secret files on certain musicians. Jim Morrison, Elvis Presley, Jimi Hendrix, Bob Marley, and many others were all in the government's files. They may even have a file on you one day." Michael winked and smiled.

"A file on me? I hope not. Why on earth would they do that?" I couldn't imagine such a thing.

"In 1968," Michael continued, "in order to prevent a riot, President Johnson called upon James Brown, a musician, to address the public after Reverend Dr. Martin Luther King Jr.

was assassinated. Mr. Brown, speaking to the masses, was able to do what no politician could; he calmed them. After that, James Brown stated that he was perceived by the government as the most dangerous man in the world. Because he did what he was asked to do, he was under close surveillance for a long time. The government felt that if he could easily stop a riot, he must easily be able to start one. Think about that. James Brown, an entertainer, was able to alter thousands of people's emotions. How did he do it? It is fascinating to think about."

That made me think about seeing James Brown in concert as a child. It was one of the most amazing concerts I've ever attended. He became my favorite performer. Holding the audience in the palm of his hand, he kept them in a frenzy. It was like being in church. I never imagined his ability could be perceived as dangerous, but now I was starting to understand.

"Church officials also know the power of Music," Michael said. "Many of them try to have the largest and best choir and band that they can. Why? Because they know that the church with the best choir has the biggest congregation. Some people pick their churches based on the quality or quantity of the Music and attend mainly for these reasons.

"Sports figures are similar to musicians. They also have a universal power to reach and affect millions. Did you know that around the year 1972 two warring countries in Africa actually called a truce for a day so that both sides could watch the soccer great Péle play a game? Think about it," he said, pointing a finger to his head. "An athlete stopped a war for a day. Most politicians can't even do that. Now that," he pointed his finger in my direction, "*that* is power.

"The only difference with sports is that competition is built in. That can cause disunity between athletes and their fans. Just as in politics, it can pit one person against another, based solely on which team each supports. Although a great athlete can cause a person to rise above this disunity, there is no built-in negative quality like that in Music."

"How can you say that?" I asked. "Music companies are always competing with each other, trying to make more money. They even fight for air time, trying to make their artists more popular than the other guys'. What about that?"

"You are talking about business, not Music," he replied. "When we attend a Music concert, we do not go in order to compete. When we put on a recording, we are not trying to win. Music is more significant than that."

Once again, he was right, and I nodded in acknowledgment.

"Imagine putting this kind of power to constructive use," he continued. "Musicians and athletes have the ability to do that. That is why it is important for the athlete to rise above the need to win. Then all fans will be on his side. You see, the competition factor is virtually nonexistent in the world of the Music fan, which allows him to express and blend his emotions without fear of ridicule or shame. Anyone who can get another person to express himself freely is powerful because he allows all involved to recognize their collective and individual power. Again, this is beautiful to some and frightening to others." He smiled and spread his hands. "Welcome to the world of the musician."

"The world of the musician." Wow, it was exciting! Hearing that information made me understand the importance and potential power of music. I thought about how I would use this kind of power if I had it. *I could be like Elvis. I could be the Bass King*, I playfully fantasized. I liked the idea of using music in a powerful way, but it bothered me that music or musicians could be frightening to anyone. I just couldn't fully understand it. The possibility of being watched by the government, the way Michael described, disturbed me. That couldn't happen in this day and age, could it? The thought of another King who had been assassinated because of his power brought me back to reality.

"Michael, I don't want to frighten anyone with my music, but I do wanna know more about 'the world of the musician.' If music really is powerful, how can I develop it to the high level you speak of? You talked about emotion. If this power is developed through emotion, how do I develop it and express it through my music in a positive way?"

"Intention!" he answered without hesitation. "Intention is the key to everything."

"What do you mean?"

"Emotions are natural. You have always had them and you will never get away from them. I look at my emotions the same way that I look at musical mistakes. Trying to get rid of them or control them can seem an impossible task. Learn to recognize and understand what they have to tell you. Only then can you effectively work with and use your emotions. How they are used is up to you. This is where intention comes in.

"Pure, honest intention can bring out the beauty of any emotion. And like notes, there is a world of beauty residing inside each one. The proper technique can bring you to the understanding and use of each emotion. Now you can start to see how the different elements of Music relate to and help each other."

"But how do I use intention?" I asked. "You haven't told me that yet."

"Just have a good heart. That is all."

I expected a more complicated answer. Michael paused in order to allow the simplicity to sink in. Sometimes he could discuss a concept for hours, and other times, just a few words did the trick. After I smiled and nodded, showing him that I understood, he continued.

"It is like trusting the river current to take you where you want to go. To fight the current could be disastrous. In each situation, whether it be in Music or in Life, take a moment to close your eyes and feel the current of your heart taking you where you need to be. After your awareness develops, you will no longer need to close your eyes. You will feel the pull of your heart's current and ride it with open eyes, allowing you to view all the astounding scenery around you. I tell you this: If you can follow the current at all times, you will not have a thing to worry about, ever."

"Ever?" I asked.

Seemingly ignoring my question, Michael rolled down the window allowing the cool fall breeze to fill the car's interior.

For the first time, I felt that he was actually taking time to think of something to say.

With his long hair fluttering out the window, he turned and asked, "Why do you practice Music?" Before I could answer, he continued. "Is your intention only to make yourself better? If so, all the forces of your being may come to help you. But if your pure intention is to make all musicians better, the same way musicians before you have done, the forces of *all* these beings may come to your aid. The spirit of Music herself will be on your side. Now listen closely." Michael leaned over and whispered in my ear. "Strive to make all Life better, and you will have all of Life's power backing you. With this power on your side, you will not have a thing to worry about, ever." He smiled and turned away, looking out the window.

We were off the highway and riding through an area called Music Row. This small area is home to most of Nashville's record labels, recording studios, and music businesses. There is even a Music Row wedding chapel. We drove by an office building with a sign that read "Creating Music is our Business."

Pointing at the sign, Michael continued his monologue. "Music is already alive. You do not create it. So if that is your intention, you are already mistaken. You cannot create Music any more than you can create a child. Music, like children, already exist somewhere in complete wholeness. Your job is to recognize that. So, in other words, you re-cognize. To 'cognize' means to become 'aware of something,' so the word 'recognize' implies that you were 'previously aware.' That is important. You help re-create the wholeness of Music by bringing it into existence on this plane. Do you understand?"

"You are throwing so many new concepts at me so fast that I don't know what I understand."

Michael chuckled. "Look at it this way. It's akin to what Michelangelo once said when asked how he created such beautiful statues. 'I did not create them,' he answered. 'They were already there. I just removed the excess marble surrounding them.'"

"I like that and I understand it," I replied. "That's a beautiful way of looking at it."

"He was a wise man," Michael said, painting with his finger in the air. "He understood, as you must, that he created nothing. If you do not re-cognize that, you are mis-taken, and you may be taken somewhere you did not intend to go. Follow the current of your heart, and you will re-member how to play musically."

He continued talking, transforming his painting finger into a conductor's baton. With both hands flailing to some unheard music, he conducted while he spoke. His tone was more playful.

"The word 'musically', broken up, becomes music-ally. That's right! Play musically, and you become an ally of Music. You actually help Music do what it is here to do. The same is true with Nature. Play and act natur-ally, and you become a Nature ally, a friend, a helper, and a contributor to Nature.

"The word 'natural' means 'having the characteristics of Nature,' but it also means 'without sharps or flats.' Now perhaps you see why I speak of Music and Nature in the same breath. They are the same thing, and it is in everyone's best interest to become their ally. Your pure intention, combined with emotion, is the best way to do that. Do you understand?"

Wow! I thought, not answering him out loud. He rarely stayed serious for so long. Maybe it was the car ride, or maybe he was just in the mood. I didn't know. I was just happy listening to him. I sat there driving with rapt attention the whole time. Even though I questioned some of his information, I didn't want to miss a word. I never knew where his knowledge came from, and I guess I didn't really care. It was all so interesting. Sometimes I knew that he would say anything just to make me think, but it was okay with me because it was working. The twenty-plus miles we'd driven seemed to fly by. In that short time he'd given me enough to think about to last a lifetime.

After we pulled up to my house and parked the car, Michael got out and picked up a rock. He held it in his hands for a few seconds and then placed it on the hood of my car. He instructed me to get four more rocks about the same size and place them on the hood of the car. I had no idea what he was going to do, but I did what he asked and waited in silence. He turned his back, closed his eyes, and told me to move the five rocks around so that they were all in different places, leaving him no way of knowing where his rock was now sitting. He asked me to make a mental note of where it was.

With his eyes still closed, he turned around, walked over to the car, and immediately picked up his rock. I was shocked. Without opening his eyes, he handed the rock back to me and asked me to rearrange the rocks again. He turned back around, and I positioned the five rocks in a different order spreading them further apart. I did it as quietly as I could. I didn't think he could tell where I was moving his rock by the sounds I was making, but who knew with this guy? To my surprise, he repeated the demonstration four more times with complete accuracy.

His ability stunned me. I couldn't begin to understand how such a feat was accomplished. I know he wasn't looking because I watched his eyes. *This guy is unreal.*

He handed the rocks to me and said, "Your turn."

"How am I supposed to do that?" I asked. Before he could answer my question with my question, I spoke again. "I know, I know. How *am* I supposed to do that?"

He just looked at me and remained silent with a slight smile on his face.

"Please!" I begged.

"Choose a rock and pour your emotions into it. Speak to it and allow it to speak to you."

Strangely, these were the only directions he gave. I looked at him for more help. He just stared back at me.

Not knowing what else to do, I picked out a rock and held it in my hands rubbing it gently, as if I was giving it a massage. I tried to muster up as many feelings as I could and pour them into the rock. I felt silly. I didn't know what I was doing and Michael knew it. After half a minute, I said I was ready. Smiling to hide my insecurity, I sat the rock down and turned around. Once the rocks were positioned, I closed my eyes and approached the car. After the pain and embarrassment of banging my leg on the car bumper wore off, I reached for my rock.

"Wrong!" he said, trying to suppress his laughter. "Again!"

I put the rock aside and reached again.

"Wrong again. Only three rocks left."

When it got down to two rocks, I finally got it right. I opened my eyes, feeling disappointed.

"Very good," he said. "Next time do it on the first try."

Before I had a chance to protest, he handed my rock back to me and instructed me to spend more time with it.

"Take all the time you need. We are in no rush. Handling emotions can be like juggling. The more balls you have, the harder it gets. This time, make it easy on yourself. Focus on one emotion at a time. Choose one emotion and work with that. Pour that one emotion into your rock with all you have."

I was still confused. How was I supposed to pour emotion into a rock? I wasn't about to ask because I knew what his answer would be. Since my mind was cluttered during my first attempt, I tried to do as he'd suggested and focus on one thing at a time. I decided to choose *love* as my emotion. But what I was supposed to do with that emotion was still unclear.

Again, as if reading my thoughts, Michael responded. "Love is the strongest of all emotions. It is also the root of all emotions. In a sense, it is what all things are made of. It is definitely what all things eventually revert back to. So using love as an emotion will allow you to blend with the very essence of the thing you are focused on."

"Love is the strongest of all emotions," was the only thing I understood. "Okay, I'll give it my best shot," I said.

I held the rock in my hands, caressing it and loving it until it began to feel warm. I kept that up for a few more minutes until, to my surprise, the rock began to feel hot. At that point I placed it on the car, turned around, and got set for the next round.

Even though I wasn't holding it, I was surprised I could still feel the rock in my hand. When Michael was ready, I closed my eyes, faced the car, and approached it with my right palm facing up as if I was still holding the rock. I slowly moved my hand, palm up, back and forth over the hood of the car. Suddenly, I felt my hand heat up. I could feel a tingling sensation running through my palm and fingers. At that point, I knew that my hand was just above my rock. I don't know how I knew, but I was sure of it, and I became excited.

As soon as I recognized my excitement, I felt a shred of doubt start to creep into my mind. Would my rock really be there when I reached for it? Did I really feel the tingling sensation? Maybe I should keep searching. The sensation in my palm started to recede. Before the doubt could totally take hold, I turned my hand over and placed it down on my rock.

"Excellent!" Michael exclaimed with a smile. "Most people would say what you just did is impossible. But you, blending your emotion of love with your palm-up technique, just communicated with a rock. What do you think about that?"

I didn't know what to say. I was proud of myself. Very proud, I might add. And for the first time, I felt that Michael was proud of me too. A spectator may have called it luck, but I knew that it wasn't.

I'd read about George Washington Carver coming up with over three hundred different uses for the peanut plant. When asked how he'd come upon his knowledge, he replied that he'd simply asked the plant. I never totally understood that story until that moment with my rock.

As we walked into the house, I could still feel the tingling in my hand. I thought about the many years I'd played my Univox bass. *There must be tons of my emotions stored in that instrument.* I wondered if I could find my bass without looking using the same technique I'd used to find my rock. I thought of many experiments that would be interesting to try. Was it luck, or was Michael really onto something? Was *I* onto something?

Michael looked at me and commented, "I tell you once again, my friend, emotion is a powerful thing. It is the force that drew me to you."

I didn't know whether he was drawn to me or I was drawn to him.

"What's the difference?" Michael replied.

I was getting used to it by then.

Dynamics

Most people play louder to get someone's attention,
but getting quieter can stop a bull from charging.

The exercise with the rock had me thinking. I'd never seen or accomplished anything like it, and I wondered how else that ability could be used. Feeling tired and excited from our morning excursion, I threw myself onto the couch.

Michael sat in the chair across from me with his eyes closed. Every so often, he would face his right palm toward the wall, slowly moving it back and forth. I knew that he lived in a different world, so I didn't pay much attention to what he was doing. I was half asleep, day-dreaming about my rock when he asked me an apparently non-related question.

"Got any Curtis Mayfield?"

"Oh yeah. CD, vinyl, 8-track—I have it all. I love Curtis Mayfield. What do you wanna hear?"

117

"A CD will do. How about *Superfly?*"

"I have that one," I replied, hopping off the couch.

"I know you do," Michael stated. "Close your eyes and find it for me."

I stopped in my tracks. "What do you mean? Close my— How am I supposed to do that?" I looked at him and frowned.

"You did it with a rock," he answered, opening his eyes to look at me.

He was right. I had done it with a rock, but I didn't know how I was supposed to do the same thing with a CD. Also, there were only five rocks to choose from. I had hundreds of CDs in my living room alone. My excitement quickly faded. I shifted my weight back and forth, trying to decide what to do. Feeling confused and frustrated, I chose to sit back down on the couch.

Ignoring my frustration, Michael gave more instructions. "This time, you should not feel for *your* emotion; you should feel for *his*."

"Whose?" I asked, tilting my head to the side.

"Curtis Mayfield's." He leaned back and closed his eyes again.

"Oh boy," I thought out loud. I fell back on the couch trying to figure out where to begin. I was lost. I tried to relate the CDs to the rocks, but it didn't help. *Maybe if I could hold the CD for a while first.* I looked at Michael. His eyes were still closed. I was about to ask for more help, but he spoke first.

Motioning toward the shelf with his finger, he commanded, "Stop thinking and go do it!"

Not trusting myself to keep my eyes closed, I picked up

a skull cap from the floor and pulled it down over my eyes. I managed to walk over to the bookshelf without bumping into anything (which, to me, was worth a treat), but I had no idea where any of my Curtis Mayfield CDs were. I also had no idea how I was supposed to find them without looking. I didn't even know if they were in that room. The thought of giving up was making its way to the forefront, but I forced it back. With no confidence on my side, I took a wild guess.

"No, that's Fleetwood Mac, *Future Games*," Michael said. "Right era, wrong group. Choose again!"

How he knew which CD I'd fingered from across the room was a mystery to me. I put the disc on the floor so I could check it later. I tried again.

"Joni Mitchell, *Shadows and Light*. Good Music, wrong CD," Michael stated.

No way! I peeked at him from under the hat. His eyes were still closed, so I looked down at the CD in my hand. He was right. How could he have known without looking? I glanced back at him and saw him smile.

"No cheating," he said, wiggling his finger. "Again!"

I tried three more times to no avail.

"Give me the hat!" Michael ordered, sounding a bit disgusted.

From his chair, he reached for the hat. I threw it at him. Without opening his eyes, he caught it and put it on, pulling it down over his eyes as I'd done. Rising from his chair, he spun around three times and then proceeded to walk backwards over to the bookshelf just to assure me that he couldn't see. Reaching the shelf, he pulled out whatever CD he wanted. It wouldn't have been that easy for me if I'd done it with my eyes open.

"The Beatles, *Abbey Road*," he stated with complete confidence. "Prince, *Dirty Mind*, Return To Forever, *No Mystery*, and Debbie Gibson, *Electric Youth*. You have a very diverse musical palette," he added with a touch of sarcasm.

He held each disc up so I could see it. I stood there stunned with my mouth wide open. He was correct each time.

"And last but not least," he said, reaching down to his right. "Curtis Mayfield, *Superfly*, the soundtrack album."

My mouth opened wider. I was more than amazed at what I'd just witnessed. It was way more astonishing than the rocks. Remember, he was blindfolded with his back to the CDs. How he knew which CD was which was beyond my comprehension.

"Shall I continue?" he asked.

Why did he have to find my Debbie Gibson CD? I knew I would never hear the end of that one. I was also secretly afraid of what else he might find. "No, no, that's enough," I answered. To feed my curiosity and hide my embarrassment, I quickly asked a question. "How did you do that?"

"I did it very well," he answered, removing the hat and taking a bow.

"Very funny. But really, can you give me a hint how you did it?"

"I can tell you exactly how I did it," he told me.

I sat on the edge of the couch poised and ready. He took his seat across from me and laid the hat in his lap. Then, folding his arms and pausing a moment, he finally began speaking.

"Earlier, when you found your rock, you tuned in to the emotions stored inside it. These were your emotions and because they were fresh, the *dynamics* were powerful, like a fresh scent to a bloodhound. With the CDs, I did the same thing, except that the emotions were not my own and the dynamics were much less then they were in the rocks; therefore, I needed to turn up my own dynamics. Emotion is stored inside Music on every CD, and even if the CD is sitting on the shelf, it can still be felt. Learning to discern the emotions of each artist is the trick."

"You tuned in to the emotions of the artists on the CD?" I asked in disbelief.

"Exactly! Have you ever noticed when you hear a song such as 'Amazing Grace,' it makes you feel different? You can tell there is something special dwelling within that song. Well, there are tons of emotions stored in there, and if you knew the origin behind that particular song, it would make complete sense to you."

I've always known that that song has a special effect on me. Every time I hear it, I feel quieter and calmer. It's similar to the feeling I get every time I take a walk in the woods.

I once heard about the composer of the song being on a ship, lost at sea. While looking at the stars, he had a revelation of some sort. That was all I knew. I wanted to know the rest of the story, but I would have to do some research. Maybe it would help me get a better understanding of what Michael was talking about.

"I am talking about vibrations and how strongly they can be felt," he said. "Most people would say that the man wrote the song, when actually, the situation he was in created it. He just happened to be aware enough to pick up on it."

"The situation wrote the song? I'll have to think about that one. What about the man? He had more to do with it than just being aware, right?" I asked.

"Of course he did. All vibrations need a conduit before they can be born, and he was it. A vibration is nothing until it has something to bounce off of. This, again, is yin yang. In order to have something, you must first have something else. The song already existed. He was the 'something else' that allowed it to exist then and there."

Whenever he talked about vibrations, I knew I would have to work hard to understand. I usually needed to revisit the information before I could completely get it, but right then, he was not waiting for me.

"Have you ever had an idea you didn't act on, only to find out later that someone else did? In other words, someone stole your idea?"

"Of course I have, many times," I answered.

"Well," he continued, "your idea is never yours alone. It's in the air for anyone to pick up. Actually, when you think about an idea, it grows stronger, making it easier for others to feel it too. Ideas create vibrations, and these vibrations can be felt in Music. 'Amazing Grace' is a perfect example."

"You can still feel the original vibrations from that song?" I asked.

"Yes. The dynamics of the original vibrations are very

faint, but because they've been upheld by other people for many years, the vibrations are still here. It is much like looking at a photograph of someone who is special to you. The age of the photograph does not matter; the person's vibrations can still be felt. Sometimes, the older the picture, the stronger the vibrations."

He walked over to the bookshelf and instantly pulled out a CD that included the song "Amazing Grace." Once again, I was surprised at his ability. Pointing to the disc, he continued speaking.

"This song is still sacred, but it doesn't mean the same thing to people that it once did."

"I do feel something from that song," I remarked, "and I know that there's more to it than a simple melody. How can I learn to be as sensitive as you are?"

"If you knew how to go inside, how to go within yourself, it would come very quickly and easily to you. That is why I urge you to pursue meditation and mind exercises. You already have a great deal of sensitivity; all people do. Maybe not enough to do what I just did, but enough to understand what I am talking about."

"I already have a great deal of sensitivity?" I asked, pointing at myself. "Then can you show me a way to develop it, please?"

"I already did."

"You did?"

"Yes, with the rock," he answered.

"Oh yeah." In the wake of Michael's astonishing exhibition with the CDs I had quickly forgotten about my own feat with the rocks. I did have a good start already. I didn't know anyone else who could do what I'd done.

"So you see, you are already well on your way." *He walked back to his chair.* "Practice that, and I will need to show you nothing else. But since I know you won't practice, I will give you another example."

I didn't know if he really knew me that well, or if he was just baiting me to start practicing. Either way, it didn't matter; I was going to get all the information I could.

"Okay, show me," I said.

"The hands," he began, rotating his open palms in the air. "The hands have a tremendous amount of sensitivity. What is the first thing you do when you get injured?" He didn't give me a chance to think of an answer. "Before you think, you touch it with your hands. It doesn't matter if it is your injury or someone else's; you just feel the urge to touch it. Why is that?" Again, he didn't wait for an answer. "It is because of an ancient memory, an instinct you have about your hands. This memory knows that your hands are sensitive and that they have a healing ability. So your hands immediately spring into action as soon as, let's say, a bee stings you. It happens before you think."

"Ancient memory? Healing? My hands have instinct? What is this nonsense you're talking about?" I cried out.

Michael quickly picked up the skull cap from his lap and threw it at my face. Without thinking, I reached up and caught it with my left hand.

"Wow!" Michael shouted. "That was awesome! How long

did you have to practice catching hats like that with your left hand before you—"

"Shut up, Michael! I get your point."

I fell back on the couch and thought about what had just happened. My left hand had just responded, instinctively, and I'm not left handed. *Maybe my hands do have a memory, and if they can remember how to protect, maybe they can remember how to heal.* I liked the thought even though I was a little upset about Michael being right again. I looked at my hands and then over at him. He was leaning back and smiling as if he were enjoying my thoughts right along with me. When I was finished, he continued speaking.

"The hands seem to have a desire of their own. They also react when you are in love. You have a desire to touch the person you are in love with. You also have a desire to touch the one you hate. Albeit in a different way," Michael chuckled, "the desire is still there.

"Children desire to touch everything too. They touch with their feet, noses, or any other part of their bodies. They love to touch. Now here is an exercise that will show you how to reach out and touch."

I sat up straight with excitement at the thought of learning something, anything, which might allow me to do as he'd done.

Michael told me to stand up and position myself about ten feet away from the stereo speakers. He said that I should stand at that close distance so I wouldn't get my emotions confused. I had no idea what he was talking about. Then he told me to turn away from the speakers, raise my right hand to about chest level, and face my palm out away from me. He placed a CD in the player and pressed *play*. It was Curtis Mayfield.

"What I want you to do," he instructed, "is slowly turn around in a complete circle. Pay attention to what you feel in your palms when you face the Music versus when you don't."

I did exactly as he asked. Now let's cut to the chase here. It worked! I felt a difference! I was shocked, and I am still shocked every time I share this exercise with someone. It works! And on my first try, as soon as I faced the speakers, I could feel a slight tingling sensation in my palm. It was faint, but I could feel it. I wasn't sure at first, if I was just feeling the actual sound waves coming from the speakers or the energy, but I could feel something.

As if reading my thoughts, Michael kept the music playing but completely turned down the volume. He asked me to repeat the exercise. He said that turning down the volume would assure me that I was feeling the emotions from the music and not the vibrations from the speakers.

It was harder to feel this time. I think my mind got in the way. It usually does after the first success, but I could still feel it, and it surprised me.

"Wow, what was that?" I asked. I was like a little boy on Christmas morning, my mouth wide open in shock.

"Emotion, Energy, Vibration, Life, Love, Music, call it what you want," he answered. "The fact that you could feel it, even when you couldn't hear it, is what's important. You now know that something is there."

"It was faint, but I felt it. I know that I did," I exclaimed, my voice revealing my excitement.

Michael spoke softly as he explained. "When vibrations are coming out faintly from an object, like speakers for instance, our first reaction may be to turn up the volume. Another approach would be to turn up our own volume, our receiving volume.

"We can turn up and down what we receive at any time. Married couples do it all the time, hearing only what they choose to hear and when they choose to hear it. This situation is similar. You adjust your own dynamics in situations when you cannot, or choose not to, adjust the dynamics of the other object."

His talk of vibrations always seemed to confuse me a bit. Even though he was now using the word dynamics, my confusion let me know that he was also talking about vibrations.

"That is why I like using Curtis Mayfield for this exercise," Michael remarked, turning up the stereo volume again. "If you notice, he plays quietly, but with a lot of intensity. There aren't many artists who can do that. Most artists think the louder they play, the more emotion there is. Actually, it is the other way around. The emotion has to be real when you are not hiding behind loud volume. And even at this quiet level," he whispered, "it would be hard for anyone not to feel the emotion coming from Curtis."

"Believe it or not, I'm following you. I actually understand what you're saying," I responded.

"Why else would I be saying it?" Michael replied. "Now, let's try it again, but in a different way this time, a way that directly relates to playing Music."

He grabbed a metronome and turned it on at about fifty beats per minute. Next, he brought over my vacuum cleaner and turned it on. (I hadn't done that in a while.) Then, he turned on the TV set and asked me to play.

"Grab your bass and play with the click," he instructed. "Play anything you want, but don't lose time with the metronome."

I had to listen really hard to hear the metronome. I could barely hear it at all until I remembered to feel for it, rather than listen for it. I amazed myself at how easy it was once I used the correct method.

"Now, turn it up," he advised. "Within yourself, raise the dynamic of the metronome."

Before I allowed myself time to think, I did what he asked. To my surprise, the click got louder. After a while, it was almost as if the television and the vacuum cleaner weren't there. Because the noise they made was constant, I was able to tune it out and play, keeping perfect time. Once I'd succeeded at that, Michael gave more instructions.

"Now try this," he said. "Instead of hearing the click on beat one, act like it is playing on the *and* of beat four. Once you can hear the click on that beat, start playing again. Also, relax your shoulders a bit."

Somehow, he could tell how tense I was. I hadn't even realized it. It was harder hearing the click on that beat, but once I took a deep breath, I could do it. Before that moment, I'd never connected my hearing to my breathing. It was a little later on that I realized I was also clearly hearing his voice in spite of all the other noise. I knew the other noise was still there, but it sounded as if it had been turned down quite a bit. Hearing the click on a different beat forced me to keep my own good time rather than rely on the metronome. It was harder to do but fortunately not impossible.

Once Michael realized that I could do it, he had me continue to change the place of the click in my mind over and over. He told me to shift the click over by a sixteenth beat each time. And each time, I had to refocus (and breathe).

After changing the click, this time to the last sixteenth of beat four, Michael asked me to solo. He said that if I could solo without losing the time, my internal clock would be solid. This would help me play with any drummer, even if his timing was bad.

I played with it a while longer, realizing how difficult it was not to lose the groove. In order to stay in time, I had to force myself to base my solo on the groove, not notes or techniques. Trying to play with the click in that unusual place also caused me to forget that the metronome was barely audible. That realization jolted me out of my groove.

"Great!" Michael said as he stopped the click and turned off the appliances. "You latched onto that one very well. You figured out how to adjust your hearing dynamics quickly while soloing. Now playing in situations where it is hard to hear will be a piece of cake, and it won't matter who you are playing with. You could use some help with your timing, but we'll get to that."

"Man, that's amazing and simple to understand," I commented.

"Oh, we haven't touched the tip of the iceberg yet," he remarked. "You wouldn't believe some of the other things you can do."

"It sounds exciting. What I would really like to see is how you use this stuff live with a band," I told him. "I would love to hear you play a gig."

"Really?" Michael asked.

"Yes, for real," I answered. "As quickly as you've helped me open up, I would love to see and hear you play in a real situation, a real gig. I'll bring the vacuum cleaner."

Michael smiled.

Just then, the phone rang. It was a musician I knew named Cliff. His band, The Cliffnotes, was very popular around town. Playing with him had helped keep me afloat when I first moved to Nashville. He always booked the highest-paying wedding gigs and somehow he was able to generate enough club dates to make many musicians want to play in his band.

He hadn't called me in a year. I didn't know why. Knowing that my rent was due and that I had no gigs lined up made me eager to take his call.

"Hey, Cliff, what's up?" I said. "Tonight?! Sure, I'm available! Okay! Thanks! Panama Red's. I'll see you at nine."

Finally, a gig. I was happy about the thought of income. It wasn't gonna pay my whole rent, but it would be a start, and maybe another gig would come out of it. I was in high spirits for a few seconds. The bottom dropped out of my excitement as soon as Michael spoke.

"I thought you wanted to hear *me* play a gig," he said.

"Well, yeah, but . . ." I didn't know what to say.

"Call Cliff back!" Michael demanded.

"What?"

"Call him back," he repeated.

"But he asked me to play," I whined.

"Call him back. It'll be okay. Just call him back."

"Okay," I answered hesitantly.

I got Cliff on the phone and told him that my teacher Michael was in town and was actually a better player than I. Even though I hadn't heard Michael play much on the bass, I recommended that Cliff hire him instead of me. Knowing how badly I needed the money, it was hard for me to do.

Cliff told me that he had double booked his band that night and was also looking for a guitar player. (Because of their popularity, he would frequently book the band in two different places at the same time and on the same night. Since Cliff was a guitar player himself, that would leave one of his bands without one.) I told him that the guitar was Michael's main instrument. To my surprise, Cliff hired us both for the same gig. Since he wouldn't be there that night, and since he hadn't heard Michael play, I assured him that all would be more than fine.

What a strange coincidence. Michael didn't seem surprised at all. He just continued to smile.

After he left my house, I battled with the anxiety I was feeling. I was both excited and nervous about playing a gig alongside of him. Not knowing how to handle these feelings, I decided to ease my mind by getting ready for the performance. It didn't work. After loading my equipment into the car, deciding what to wear became the next challenge. I felt a headache coming on. Not knowing what to do, I sat down trying to relax. I wondered if Michael was going through the same dilemma. After a short break, I left for the club wearing the clothes I'd had on all day.

Wanting to look really dedicated, I showed up two hours early. Most of The Cliffnotes' gigs are very laid back, so showing up that early is uncommon. I was the first one there. When Ralph, the drummer, arrived, we talked and caught up for a while. I made up a story about why he hadn't seen me gigging around town lately and acted as if I was interested in what he'd been up to. I spent the next fifteen minutes trying to explain who the weird guy was walking through the door carrying a skateboard and a guitar.

Michael was dressed as usual—that is, unusually. I couldn't remember the last time I'd seen a pair of knickerbockers. He wore a different color sandal on each foot with checkered socks up to the knee. A hole in each sock allowed his big toe to stick out, securing his sandals to his feet. I guessed that he'd left his shirt at home, because he wasn't wearing one. His long flowing hair hung down, partially covering his suspenders.

His guitar, well, it wasn't his. It was mine, the one that served as a coat rack in my living room. I hadn't realized he'd taken it. Maybe he'd grabbed it from the house after I'd already left. I knew that he didn't need my key to get in. Rather than upset me it made me chuckle.

How he could waltz in dressed like that, carrying my beat-up guitar without a case, was bewildering. I secretly wished I could be so bold, but I knew that I'd never be. *Michael has enough boldness for both of us.*

After the rest of the band arrived, we introduced ourselves to one another. It's not uncommon to show up for a gig of this type and not know many, or any, of the other musicians you are about to play with.

My equipment was set up on the hi-hat side of the drummer, so Michael set up to my left. Fortunately the club had a guitar amp for him to use. I wondered if he was unprepared or if he'd somehow known the amp would be waiting for him.

The sax player was warming up by religiously playing scales and practicing his fingerings. I pulled out my bass to do the same. Michael was sitting there reclined in a wooden chair with his feet resting on the stage. His eyes were closed. His guitar was lying on the table.

"Don't you need to warm up?" I asked him.

"Do you?" he replied, looking up at me.

"Yes, I do."

"How long you been playing?" he asked.

"About twelve years, or so."

"And you're not warmed up yet?" With that comment, he closed his eyes again.

"I want to be ready for tonight's gig. It's important to me," I answered.

"I have been warming up my whole Life for this gig," Michael explained with his eyes still closed. "It's an important one for me also. All the previous gigs were just rehearsals for tonight. It all leads to now."

I didn't know what to say. I also didn't know whether I should continue warming up or not. The sax player overheard our short conversation. He stopped playing, walked over, and made a snide comment to Michael.

"Dude, you might wanna pick up your axe before the gig starts. I don't want you warming up on my time."

The sax player obviously didn't know who he was dealing with. I would've tried to save him if I'd had the time or the inclination. I awaited Michael's response.

"I see," Michael said, slowly sitting up in his chair. I could tell by his smile that he was going to enjoy this interaction. He stood up, which allowed him to look down on the sax player. Staring him straight in the eyes, he continued speaking.

"You're warming up with your fingers because that's all you use when you play. I can already hear it. Me, I use my mind. We can compare notes after the gig if you want. You let me know. I'll be right here."

Michael sat back down, propped up his feet, and closed his eyes again, waiting a while before letting his grin fade. I knew it was on purpose.

The sax man was perplexed. Michael's words had stopped him in his tracks. He just stood there not knowing what to do. I could see him thinking about it, but he didn't dare try to argue although I silently hoped he would. I wanted to see Michael in action. *Maybe after the show*, I hoped.

The rest of the band came over to talk about a few songs. Once the set list was confirmed, the music began.

The first few songs went by rather smoothly, and I was feeling good about my playing. But eventually, I noticed that the people in the bar weren't listening. That had always been a pet peeve of mine, and it started to bother me. Michael didn't seem to notice or maybe he just didn't care, but it was already getting the best of me. Finally, he spoke.

"Do you see that guy talking at the far end of the bar?" he asked. "He's wearing a white jacket."

"Yes," I answered.

"Watch him."

Everyone at the bar was talking. The only people listening were the few people on the dance floor. The rest were either sitting at the bar or at a table, not listening. I didn't know what I was looking for or what Michael was planning to do. I just kept watching the man in the white jacket.

Almost immediately, the man turned and looked at the stage. *Someone noticed the band. This is a first.* Less than a minute later, he picked up his drink and walked to the front of the room taking a seat at a table almost directly in front of Michael. He wasn't looking at him, but that's where he sat. Michael turned to me and smiled.

I was baffled. I wasn't sure if he had caused the man to sit there or not. Maybe he could read lips and overheard the man's plans to sit up front. Unlikely. I knew that Michael was strange, and by now I was pretty sure that he had something to do with all the strange things that happened around him.

"How did you do that?" I asked (losing the beat in the process). Ralph looked at me and frowned. I gave an apologetic glance in return.

"On the break; wait 'til the set break. I'll explain then," Michael told me.

I could hardly wait for the first intermission. Most bands take more breaks than I'm used to, so when it came time to stop, I was ready but also surprised that it came so soon.

"Okay Michael, fill me in," I said, not even waiting for him to unhook his strap.

"Dynamics," he replied. "I used dynamics."

"Can you teach me to do that?" It wasn't until after I'd asked the question that I remembered his outlook on "teaching."

"Can you learn how to do that? That is a better question," he answered.

"Yeah, yeah, teach me, show me, learn me, blah blah blah. How can *I* do that? That's all I wanna know." That made him laugh. We walked outside where it was quiet, and there, he filled me in on his method.

"All right, here's what I did. It was obvious that the guy wasn't listening to Music, so I needed to get his attention. All I did was alter the dynamics of my playing. Not just the volume but also the dynamics of all the elements. That got his attention. If you noticed, he glanced at the stage a few times before making his way up there. Once I knew I had him, I turned up the dynamics. Again I'm not just talking about volume. My volume actually got softer. That's what drew him in. You see, most people play louder to get someone's attention, but getting quieter can stop a bull from charging."

"That's downright amazing," I said.

"No, it's even better than that," he answered. "That guy had no idea what attracted him to the stage. If he knew anything about our world of Music, he would have noticed what

I did and would have paid direct attention to me. Because he didn't know what hit him, I was able to influence his thinking. This is both awesome and dangerous for both parties involved. If you can do it to him, it can be done to you. Think about it. We are only dealing with Music in this situation."

I didn't totally understand what he was talking about, but one phrase caught my attention. "You said 'our world of music.' Are you including me in your world?" My eyebrows rose as I smiled a hopeful smile.

"Yes! You must be a part of this world to manipulate the elements in that way."

I felt proud to be included in his world but chose not to show it. "I see. Can you show me how to manipulate the elements in that way?" I asked.

"It's easy," he answered. "I'll show you how to make the audience applaud for whomever is soloing. They will go crazy for the soloist without realizing it was you who caused them to do it."

That sounded way cool to me. "You have got to show me how to do that." I was ready to get on my knees if I had to, and Michael knew it.

"Who's the best?" he asked, opening his arms and raising one eyebrow in a playful manner.

"You are, Michael. You are."

"Who do you love?" The familiar, knowing smile was now showing.

"You, okay? Now stop it and tell me what to do."

It was a rare thing to hear Michael joke in that way. He never asked for affection or seemed to care about it. Even though I could tell he was joking, I was willing to do anything in order to learn what he had to teach.

"Okay, now I'll show you," he said with a chuckle. "It's so easy. Here's what you do. When we go back up there and the horn player starts to solo, pay attention to when he's about to peak. Before he does, I want you to go up two octaves and 'pedal' a note."

(Pedaling a note is when the bass player stays on one note, repeating it over and over, even though the chords may be changing. Got it? Okay, back to the story.)

"As you pedal the note," he continued, "you must bring the volume down really low. Bring the volume down without losing the intensity. Think Curtis Mayfield. The drummer needs to follow you with this dynamic, so you may need to get Ralph's attention. Pedal the note for eight to sixteen measures. How long is up to you, but it must be timed correctly in order for it to work. Direct your full attention to the horn player as you do it. Draw no attention to yourself.

"During the last two to four measures, your intensity should grow. I want you to crescendo as you descend, working the notes back down to the original octave. Then start playing your original bass line again, grooving real hard. At that point, if you've done it correctly, the audience will start applauding for the soloist. You can take credit for it on the inside, but on the outside, the credit goes to the soloist. In other words, you keep quiet about what you've done. This quiet world is the world you live in as a bass player."

"That sounds easy," I said, excited to try it. "Basically, I pedal a note for a few bars, then walk back down and start playing the groove again, right?"

"Yes, but you can't forget about the dynamics. You must bring the volume down and back up at the appropriate times. This is crucial in order for it to work."

"Okay, I'll try it and see if it works when we get back up there."

"No! Don't *try* it! *Do* it and make it work! You can work out the kinks right now in your mind if you want to, but when we're up there on the stage, it will be time to make it work. 'I don't want you rehearsing on my time.'" He spoke the last line loud enough for everyone to hear. The sax player gave a glance but dared not comment.

After a quiet chuckle, I closed my eyes and thought through the whole process. I could hear the music in my mind and realized that if I pulsated between two notes while pedaling, it would be easier for me to make it groove, even at a low volume. I was excited and couldn't wait to try it. I mean, I couldn't wait to *do* it.

When we hit the stage, we started with an instrumental piece. Once the sax player started soloing, I listened intently, planning my attack. *This is the perfect time.* As soon as he started his third chorus, I dove in, pedaling the root note and the minor seventh, two octaves up. I hadn't told Michael that I was going to use two notes, but when I did, he gave me an approving nod.

I brought the volume way down, and Ralph followed. Michael stopped playing chords and went to a single note rhythm that really created space. It was then that I realized what we were doing. We were creating a hole right in the middle of the music that allowed the soloist to stand there out in the open. We also simplified the music, directing all of the attention to the soloist. The sax player was standing there in the middle of a musical vacuum, and the audience had to take notice. They really did. The whole audience stopped what they were doing and started listening to the saxophone solo. It was brilliant.

After the appropriate amount of time, I started bringing the volume back up. Again, Ralph followed. As we executed the perfect crescendo, I started walking down the scale notes of the song until I landed firmly on the root and resumed the original groove in prodigious fashion. I could feel the effect of what was happening.

Everyone in the room burst into thunderous applause, including the waitresses and bartenders. In between chords, Michael gave me a shot in the arm to show his approval. He was smiling heavily at me. The rest of the audience continued clapping and cheering for the sax player who was more inspired than he'd been all night. He soloed for two more choruses and you could almost see the joy coming through his skin.

The audience was leaving the bar to fill the seats up front. They were listening, they were on our side, and the band felt it. The rest of the night was one of the best I've had in Nashville. I felt as if it was the start of something good.

Once the gig was over, a lady named Jonell came over and told me that she liked my playing. I'd noticed her in the club but didn't know who she was. She was a beautiful, short, auburn-haired lady who looked like she could hold her own, somewhat of a cross between Janis Joplin and Bonnie Raitt. She mentioned that she was looking for a bass player to sub in her band for a few nights. I told her that I was available, and we exchanged numbers. Later Michael told me that she was one of the best singers in the country. I made a mental note to contact her sooner rather than later.

I hadn't felt so good in ages, but I also felt that I owed it all to Michael. When I mentioned that to him, he refused all credit.

"Twenty years from now," he said, "this knowledge will be looked upon as your own. Therefore, it should be looked upon now as your own."

"But this gig wouldn't have happened this way if it weren't for you," I told him. "I don't think it would've happened at all if it weren't for you. So I thank you for it."

"Thank me all you want, but don't give me credit for what you've done. You played well tonight, and it is *you* I thank."

"Thank me for what?" I asked.

"For making me proud," he answered.

It almost sounded cliché, but it touched me deeply, for I could tell that he was sincere. I couldn't think of anything else to say, and it didn't seem quite appropriate to give him a hug in front of the guys, so I just answered, "You're welcome."

We walked over to the bar where the other band members were sitting. Although they had packed up their equipment, they couldn't leave; they were still energized from the gig. Oh yeah, we were also still waiting for the owner to pay us.

The whole band was excited. They commented on how much they enjoyed playing with Michael and me. Ralph told me that he would make sure Cliff knew how well we had done. That made me feel great, and I hoped it meant more gigs.

The sax player apologized to Michael for his earlier attitude and told him that he hoped to play with him again sometime. Michael thanked him and suggested that he remember to use his mind, not just his fingers. Michael glanced at me and winked.

Sometime later, I played another gig with the same horn player. After doing his usual warm-up routine, I saw him take a seat in the corner and close his eyes. *Using his mind.* Michael had a way of influencing everybody he came in contact with.

Once we got paid, we noticed Michael was nowhere to be found. I let them know that I would probably be seeing him in the morning. His money was given to me to pass on to him. I was accustomed to Michael showing up unexpectedly, but it was strange for him to disappear in such a fashion. Since we hadn't arrived together, I decided not to worry about him and walked to my car. As I arrived, I found Michael sitting on the hood.

"I knew you wouldn't take it if I gave it to you, so I allowed them to give it to you," he said.

"What are you talking about?"

"You know what I'm talking about," he answered.

"What? I'm not taking your money. It's for you."

"I don't need it; you do. Plus, it's already in your pocket.

Keep it; you earned it tonight. If I ever need it, I know where you live."

"I can't do that," I told him.

"Listen, at this point in my journey, Music is Life, and I do not need money to play it or live it. Money is not something I play for anymore. It used to be at one time, but now I play for other reasons. Tonight, I played for you. And the way that you played, you've already paid me well."

I didn't know how to respond. "Thank you, Michael. You are incredible."

"No, I am better than that!" He smiled, turned, and walked away.

I longed to be at his level. As strange as he was, he was the most *real* person I knew. I couldn't imagine anyone else who would've done for me what he had done. I knew that he was sincere about everything he'd said, and it touched me deeply on many different levels.

"That is true dynamics," I whispered to myself.

Feeling emotional, I watched him ride off into the moonlight—on his skateboard.

Rhythm/Tempo

If you pay attention correctly,
it won't matter if you're in another room or in
another state, you'll still be able to feel the pulse.

I woke up with a headache. Trying to assimilate all the new knowledge was taxing my brain. Although I was tired, sleep had eluded me for the majority of the night. I was so excited about what I was learning that I couldn't get it off my mind. Anytime Michael introduced a new idea, it sparked another one. This new idea would then spark yet another one, and so on. My brain, not wanting to waste time with sleep, caused me to stay up later than I was used to. I'm sure it was all part of his design.

I went to the kitchen to get myself a glass of orange juice. Most people start their day with a cup of coffee, but me, I have to have a glass of orange juice. I've never had a taste for coffee or alcohol, but if they ever start an Orange Juicers Anonymous organization, I will have to be the president. I opened the refrigerator and it was empty—no orange juice. I would have to go to the nearest store if I was going to get my fix.

It was early, at least for me. If I were the type to wear pajamas, I would've still been wearing them. Instead, I wore my usual sweat pants and t-shirt. Normally, I don't like going out first thing in the morning because 'first thing in the morning' starts about four hours later for me than it does for other people. When the sun is almost straight overhead, people expect you to at least *look* like you've been awake for a while.

I'd only been gone for about twenty minutes, so you can imagine my surprise when I walked back into *my* house and saw a little boy sitting on *my* couch holding *my* bass guitar. Believe it or not, my first instinct was to apologize for the mess, but then I remembered that he was just a little boy.

I looked around to see who he was with and found it puzzling that he was alone. I didn't know what to think. He looked like a nice kid, short and skinny with dark hair that was both bushy and wavy. He also wore glasses. It was obvious to me that both his pants and shirt were ironed and his shoes were spotless, unlike the beat-up sneakers most kids his age wore. He looked like the geeky kid who gets picked on in school.

The kid watched me with a smile on his face as I continued to look him over, trying to figure him out. He didn't appear to be lost. He just sat there with the confidence of someone who knew where and who he was. For some reason, I also felt that he was where he was supposed to be. Kindness, no—politeness, if there is a difference, seemed to radiate from him. That eased my mind.

"Who are you?" I asked.

"Michael said you needed help with your timing," he answered, still smiling. "I hope you don't mind that I was playing your bass."

"What's your name?"

"Sam, sir."

"How old are you, Sam?"

"I'm eleven," he answered.

"Eleven? Michael sent an eleven-year-old boy to help me with my timing?"

"Yes, sir," he answered matter-of-factly, still smiling.

"Well, um, okay then." I was really at a loss for words. "You want a beer?" I joked.

"No, thank you," he answered, ignoring my failed attempt at humor. "But I will take a glass of orange juice. You should have a cup of water; it'll help you with your headache." His high-pitched voice was as polite as any I'd ever heard.

I brought the bag into the kitchen and poured us each a tall glass of juice. Letting a kid tell me what to drink was not my intention, but this kid was cute. Then it hit me. How did he know about my headache? I was used to that kind of stuff from Michael, but from an eleven-year-old? The kid was intriguing. I didn't really want the juice anymore, but I drank it anyway just to prove a point.

Walking back into the living room I asked, "Can you play?"

"A better question is can *you* play?" he answered, still smiling.

"I see that you've been hanging around Michael. What are you here to *show* me?" I asked, emphasizing the word 'show,' to let him know I'd been around Michael a bit too.

"I wanna help you with your timing, but first I think we should deal with your headache."

"We?" I asked.

"Yeah, I'll help you with it if you'd like me to."

"All right," I answered, more to appease him than because I believed him.

"Okay, the first thing you need to do is smile."

I wasn't about to smile. His constant smile was already starting to irritate me. I frowned instead.

"Michael told me that you would act this way," he commented.

"Like what?" I asked.

"Like a donkey. Michael used a different word that I'm not allowed to say, but I think he meant 'stubborn.'" He started to laugh. "He said you'd rather keep the headache than risk learning something from a kid. Too much pride, I guess."

Now it seemed Michael also knew I had a headache. Did he have the kid programmed? I stood there trying hard not to let the eleven-year-old confuse me. I could feel myself getting angry. Not knowing what else to do, I decided to see what the boy had to offer. There was no one around to witness it if he happened to be much smarter than I, so I decided to give in to him.

"Okay, Sam, what do you want me to do?"

"Smile! Really, just smile. Think of something nice or funny that will make you smile, but it has to be real. It will help slow down your *tempo* a bit. Tempo and temper are related, you know."

The kid seemed to know what he was talking about, so I decided to give it a try. I thought about the time that I saw Michael perform three cartwheels in my living room. It was in response to my finally understanding a concept of his that I was having trouble with. He told me it was what a child would've done. Watching him maneuver his tall frame around the furniture in my small living room was a sight to behold. That memory made me laugh.

"Great," Sam said. "Now, how do you feel?"

"I have to admit, I do feel a little better," I answered.

It was the truth. Smiling immediately relieved much of the tension. The headache wasn't completely gone, but the throbbing in my temple had slowed down. It was tolerable. If I had to spend the rest of the day feeling like this, I could do it. That thought caused me to smile even more. Of course Sam was still smiling, but now it didn't bother me as much.

"That's always the first thing you should do whenever you wanna feel better. It works for anything, even nervousness or stage fright," he revealed. "It's also infectious—people around you will start to smile too."

"I'll have to remember that. I don't get stage fright, but I will try it for everything else."

"Oh, you will," he said.

I wasn't sure what he was referring to, so I let it go. "What should I do next?" I asked.

"You should bless your headache."

"What?"

"Bless it," he repeated. "Appreciate what it's telling you. That's important."

"What do you mean 'bless it?' I don't want this headache. I didn't ask for it, and I surely don't want to bless it. I don't know what it's telling me, but I'm telling you that you need to spend more time with that friend of yours because this time, kid, you are wrong."

Still smiling, he proved me wrong. "Maybe you didn't ask for it, but you should be grateful for it. It's an indicator."

"A what?" I asked.

"When your car starts to run out of gas, a little indicator light comes on as a warning. That's a blessing. Your attitude toward the light should be an attitude of gratitude. You don't get mad and wanna tear it up, do you? You don't wanna take something to make it go away either. You're happy that the light gave you the warning, right? You also know that if you don't pay attention to the warning, you might have a bigger problem.

"So what we need to do is treat your headache like that little light. When your headache shows up, you should first be thankful for it. Know that it's here as an early warning; then deal with it right away. In other words, if your timing is right, you can erase the problem before it becomes one. Cool, huh?"

"Once I recognize the warning signs, how do I get rid of the headache?" I asked him. The kid was making sense, and I was interested in hearing what else he had to say.

"You need to figure out what it's warning you about. What's the cause? It's not enough to recognize the signs; you have to get to the root of the problem. I hear that you have problems finding the root." He winked his left eye and flashed a Michael-esque grin. "Now sometimes the root may be buried way down deep, but it must be dug up; it must be exposed so that it can be worked on and prevented in the future.

"In this case, it's easy. You just need to drink more water and less juice. In other cases, the causes may be much deeper than that. You may have to deal with them in stages. The main point is that you gotta deal with 'em."

"Okay, you say that I need to drink more water. Is that the cause of my headache? Will drinking some water make it go away?"

"Maybe it will; maybe it won't. That's up to you. But even if it doesn't, you should still be happy that your indicator light came on. Then you should thank it."

"Thank it?" I asked with perhaps more belligerence than I should have. "Thank my headache?"

"Sure!" Smiling Boy replied. "If it weren't for your headache, you might not know that your body was dehydrated until it was too late. So yes, you should be thanking and blessing your headache right now. That's what I think."

For some reason, maybe because no one else was around, I decided to try it. I told my headache I was proud and happy that it acted as an early warning system. I thanked it for showing up and for gently nudging me back on track. I also welcomed it to return anytime I needed it to. It actually felt really good to thank my headache. And to my surprise, after I was finished, my headache was gone.

"How do you feel?" Sam asked.

"I feel great! My headache is gone!" I exclaimed.

Without hesitation, Sam got up and did three cartwheels around my living room just as I'd seen Michael do. His small frame twirled around so fast that I nearly missed the display. How he did it without knocking anything over in such a tiny space was pretty amazing. Then it hit me. Had I thought about Michael doing cartwheels out loud, or had Sam...? Wait, how did he know? *I don't know about this boy*, I thought to myself, or was it only to myself?

"A headache can teach us a lot about timing," Sam said after finishing his exhibition.

"How so?" I asked.

"They come at the perfect time. Imagine if they showed up after our bodies broke down."

"I guess you're right."

"And speaking of timing..." He paused and reached into his book bag.

Hearing his gentle, high-pitched voice reminded me that I was dealing with a kid, but I also realized that it no longer bothered me. Pride had receded.

From his bag, he pulled out a drum machine and plugged it into a spare channel on my bass amp. Without turning it on, he handed me the bass and instructed me to play.

"Play what?" I asked.

"He told me you'd say that too," the youngster commented. "Play anything. Play something you'd play with a band."

I thought for a moment and then played a familiar pattern. Sam interrupted me rather quickly.

"I can tell you've played that lick, like, a zillion times, right?"

Of course he was right. "Yes I have," I sheepishly replied.

"Okay then, stop thinking about it. Your *rhythm* is all screwed up. You've been playing the bass guitar and that lick long enough that you shouldn't have to think about 'em anymore. If you have to think about 'em all the time, it will show up in your playing. And if you continue to play only your bass and your licks, when will you ever get to play Music?"

"Wow! Are you sure you're only eleven?" I asked, not expecting an answer. It was a good point, a great point actually. "What should I think about then?" I asked.

"Well for now, think about your timing because when you're playing by yourself, it's not that good. When you play with a drummer, it *is* good. So I recommend that you hear the drummer as you play. Even before you play, hear the drummer in your head. Do that for a few bars before you begin this time."

Taking his advice, I imagined a drummer playing a steady beat. When I was ready, I played along. This time, even *I* could tell it was better. It felt good. I could see Sam bouncing his head to the beat like a little dark-haired bobble-head doll. Then I hit a wrong note and my attention went back to the bass. Sam heard it too.

"No!" he cried out. "For this exercise, keep your full attention on the drummer. You don't need to think about the bass at all, even when you play a wrong note."

I did that for a while longer, following Sam's gentle instructions. He also gave me other things to experiment with. At one point, he asked me to imagine an explosion going off on the first beat of each measure, assuring me that it would surely lock me into the rhythm. It did.

Sam suggested that when I'm on a gig, I should divide my attention between myself and the rest of the band, but for these specific exercises, all attention should go to the focus points he was giving me.

The young man then turned on the drum machine which he'd already programmed with a four bar pattern. He instructed me to play and told me to stick to a simple groove, not to solo. I did that until he felt I was comfortable. Then he made a change on the machine. He played the same pattern, but this time, the fourth bar was completely empty. For one bar of the pattern, I was playing without the drums. This was to see how steady I could hold the time by myself and then come back in on beat one. The machine would let me know if I was correct or not.

Once I'd succeeded at that, Sam repeated the exercise two more times, first leaving out bars three and four, and then leaving out bars two, three, and four. That left me with only one full measure to find the rhythm and three measures to hold on to it. He allowed me to get comfortable with each phase, as the exercise became progressively more difficult.

"Even though the drums are not playing," he told me,

"the pulse is still there. You gotta grab onto that pulse as quickly as you can and lock it into your body. It's really important that you do that. Then you'll feel where you need to be at all times."

I knew what he was talking about. When playing with a good drummer, the pulse can easily be felt. Even though different drummers have different pulses, I still agreed with Sam. If *I* was really "in the groove," I would definitely be able to feel the pulse.

"Now I'll make it just a little bit harder," he said. "This will tell us how 'locked in' you really are."

He changed the drum machine once more. There were still four measures playing, but there was an audible beat programmed to play on beat one only. I only had one beat out of sixteen to grasp the tempo. *He can't be serious,* I thought. He was. A bit intimidated, I closed my eyes and listened closely.

To my surprise, I could do it. I could still feel the pulse and I locked in to it. It was a little strange. Even though there was no audible pulse playing, I could definitely feel it. With just one beat to go on, I kept perfect time for the next fifteen beats. I was so happy that I felt like doing three cartwheels myself. I opened my eyes to find Sam fiddling with the drum machine once again. He changed it back to the original program consisting of four complete patterns.

"Now we'll start all over," he continued. "Play the same groove, but this time start adding in some 'fills' at the end of measures."

It was pretty easy until the drum machine started leaving

out measures. It was then that I realized where my focus went whenever I played a fill. I rushed like crazy during every one of them, and the drum machine let me know it. Sam pointed out that during my fills, my attention would revert back to the bass and the groove would falter because of it. That was a "big no-no." "Remember," he said, "for this exercise, keep your focus on the pulse, not on what you're playing."

When I succeeded at each phase of the exercise, he started the whole process over again, this time instructing me to "all out solo." It was difficult. Trying to figure out what to play and keep the pulse was easier said than done. I did well at the beginning stages of the exercise, but when it got down to having only one beat out of sixteen, I was completely lost.

Raising his hand to stop me, Sam spoke. "When you get to the place where you can solo to just one beat every four measures and not lose the pulse, playing with a drummer, even a bad drummer, will be a piece of cake. Here, let me show you."

He picked up my bass and played a very solid groove to the pattern consisting of only one beat. I was shocked. This eleven-year-old boy could play, and he smiled the whole time. *Maybe that's the key.* If it worked on my headache, maybe it could work on my groove.

He then proceeded to play the best bass solo I'd heard in a long time. He started with a sixteenth note pattern leaving a space on beat one just so I would know he was right on it. He didn't deviate from the pulse even a little. Just when I thought it couldn't get any better, Sam took it to another level.

"There's one more level to the 'one beat' part of this exercise," Sam told me. "It's an advanced level. You're not ready for it, but I'll show it to you anyway if you'd like."

"I can't imagine anything more amazing than what you just did, but yes, please show me."

"Before, when we were playing, we were focused on feeling the pulse," he said. "It was feeling the pulse that allowed us to stay in time. Now the goal will be to lose the pulse altogether. Let's not focus on it. I'll try my best to have no idea where it is. I'll allow the feeling in my body to tell me how much space has gone by; then I'll make a guess and see if I can play on beat one."

He resumed playing to the one-beat-only pattern on the drum machine. At first he allowed his amazing groove to take over, but then he started playing random patterns in no particular rhythm. He was talking to me at the same time. Every time beat one came around, he was right on it. It was pretty amazing, but it was nothing compared to what he was about to show me.

"Turn the volume all the way down," he instructed. "There's a blinking light on the machine that'll tell you where beat one is. I won't look at it, but I'll still try to keep time with it. Let me know how I do."

I did what he asked when all of a sudden, he put the bass down and walked into the kitchen. My eyes darted between him and the drum machine. I didn't know what he planned to do. I could hear him pouring himself a glass of orange juice. Except for the sound of juice hitting the glass, it was silent in the room. Then, from the kitchen I heard him shout,

"One!" I was looking at the light on the drum machine and he was right with it. It was unbelievable. It is still unbelievable. His voice and the blinking light were completely in sync.

I watched as he walked down the hallway and into the bathroom. He relieved himself and flushed. After washing his hands, he again shouted, "One!" It seemed impossible. If I wasn't witnessing it, I would've never believed that anyone's timing could be that good. Returning to the living room, he took a seat next to me on the couch. He looked directly into my eyes as Michael had done many times before. For once, he wasn't smiling.

His voice lowered. "Music is alive, and if you treat her that way, she will speak to you. You will feel her pulse. That is her heartbeat. If you pay attention correctly, it won't matter if you're in another room or in another state, you'll still be able to feel it."

As he talked, Sam appeared much older. His voice took on the tone of someone much wiser than his age allowed. I listened carefully as he continued.

"It doesn't have to take long to learn what I just did. Music is played from the mind, not the body. So do whatever you can to exercise your mind. That's very important! Okay?" With that comment he stood up to leave.

I was in awe. "Shouldn't you be in school?" I joked.

"This is school, isn't it?" he answered, smiling again. He then turned and walked away.

As I watched him close the door, I sat there amazed at the little kid who had just given me a music lesson. Even though I was a bit embarrassed at the situation, I wished that someone else had been there to witness what I'd just been through. I knew that no one would believe me if I told them. I sat back on the couch trying to remember all that Sam had shown me.

As I started to get up to get myself a glass of water, I realized that he'd left his drum machine. How would I ever find him to return it? I didn't know who he was or where he lived. I looked at the machine and noticed it was still running. Just then, I heard the door open. It was Sam.

"One!" he shouted, just as the light blinked. "You can keep it. Thanks for a really fun day, sir. Timing is everything, isn't it?"

I sat, stunned and silent.

Tone

Doctors use lasers to operate. Music,
in the right hands, can do the same thing.

It was later that day, after Sam had left, that I was driving downtown. I hadn't seen Michael all day and was hesitant to leave my house for fear of missing him. I had a few questions about Sam I wanted to clear up. He told me that he had learned from Michael about twelve years earlier. Since he was only eleven, that statement raised a few questions in my mind.

I was driving through a pretty run-down part of town when I saw someone who resembled Michael. I drove around the block to get another look, and sure enough, it was him. He was sitting in the grass talking to a homeless man. Michael's clothes were more tattered and worn than I'd ever seen them. He looked like a homeless man himself. I wasn't sure he wanted me to see him that way, but just as I decided to drive on by, he stood up and flagged me down. I parked the car, locked the door, and walked over to him.

"It tooks ya long enough. I thought you neva was gonna show up," Michael said.

"You thought what?" I asked. I never knew if he was serious when he said stuff like that, or if he was just improvising. I decided that it didn't matter. Also, his new dialect was confusing me.

"Dis is Uncle Clyde." he said. "He's originally from New Awleens, but he lives over dere unda da bridge now. We sits here ever so often just talkin' 'bout dis and dat. Right now we's tryin' to figure out if'n Life is alive or not. I says dat it is, and so do Clyde. We jus' trying to figure out a way dat anyone can say dat it's not."

Uncle Clyde was an older man. He seemed much older than Michael, but since I didn't know Michael's age, Clyde's age remained a mystery too. His skin was dark, as was his short scruffy hair. His graying mustache and full beard hid both his top and bottom lips but didn't totally obscure his peaceful smile. Although he appeared elderly, his skin was smooth and his teeth were straight and white.

His demeanor was not like that of most homeless people. He seemed happy and cheerful, as if he was exactly where he wanted to be. And unlike other homeless people I'd seen in the area, he carried nothing with him. He had no bag or cart heaped with his possessions. His clothes, though tattered, were not dirty, just very worn, as if he wanted them that way.

"You mus be dat musician Michael wus tellin' me about," Uncle Clyde said. "He say dat you's real good, but dat you don't know it yet. Come 'ere and let me have a look atcha."

I glanced at Michael.

"Goes on, son. It's awright," Michael added, gesturing toward Uncle Clyde.

I could understand Clyde talking that way, but it was awkward hearing Michael speak in such a manner. If I'd heard that voice over the phone, I wouldn't have believed it was him.

I walked over to where Uncle Clyde was sitting. He slowly rose to his feet as if every bone in his body ached and proceeded to look me over. The way he moved made me think that I should be examining him instead.

He started by looking closely at individual strands of my hair. He even pulled out a strand (which hurt by the way) and showed it to Michael. They talked about it for a moment, but I couldn't hear what they said.

He then worked his way down my body, examining everything from my eyes down to my feet. I even had to remove my shoes for him. "Wear clean socks and underwear, son. You never know when a homeless man is gonna give you a physical," I could hear my mom saying. I looked at Michael during the long process. He assured me with his looks that I should let Clyde continue.

When he was done, Uncle Clyde looked at Michael and said, "I thinks dat if da word life means dat sumpin' is alive, den dat mus mean dat Life is alive."

"Makes complete sense to me," Michael replied.

"Wait a minute," I interrupted impatiently. "Aren't you gonna tell me what you found out?"

"About wut?" they asked in unison.

"About me! You just looked over my whole body from head to toe. Aren't you gonna tell me anything about it?"

Michael looked at Uncle Clyde and I did the same.

"Well suh, I don't rightly care about yo' body too much," Clyde said as he lowered himself back to the ground. "I wus jus' lookin' at it to see 'bout you. I jus' wanted to see if'n you is what Michael says you is. You know how he can stretch da trufe sometimes."

I knew what he was talking about, but it wasn't the time to discuss Michael's truth stretching. I was more curious about other things. "What did my body tell you about me?" I asked.

"Well suh, if'n you really wanna know, I guess it's alright to tell ya a thing or two. You think so, Michael?" He glanced at Michael for his approval. Michael nodded in affirmation.

"Yo' body," said Clyde, "resonates wit a certain vibration. Dis vibration puts out a certain *tone* dat I can read, dependin' on what yo' soul is up to, dat is. Sorta like how an engineer can read da tones in Music. You see, yo' soul has an agenda fo' you. Now even you don't know wut dat agenda is, I can see dat, but you and yo' soul is just about to catch up wit' each other. It's always exciting when dat happens in a person's Life. Fo' some people, it happens before dey gets here. Dat ain't no fun at all. Dis is where da fun is at. I wanna see you again in a few years." He turned to look at Michael.

"I know dat's right," Michael commented. They shared a laugh.

"You know about music too, Uncle Clyde?" I asked. I didn't know why I was asking about music when he was telling me such interesting things about myself.

"Oh yeah, son. I plays Music, and one day when you realize how ta stop jus' playin' yo' bass, you's gonna start playin' Music too."

Stop playing my bass? That was the second time that day someone had talked about that. What did it mean? I was just about to ask when Michael butted in.

"Uncle Clyde is the best harmonica player on the planet, in my opinion," he said.

"Yes I is, but we ain't here ta talk about me, is we?" Clyde answered. "But jus' ta let yous in on a lil' secret, I knows a lil' bit about everathang. So do you. Dats wut you's about to find out."

"Dat's wut I'm about to—I mean, that's what I'm about to find out? What does that mean?" I asked.

"It don't mean nuthin' to you yet," he answered. "In due time, son, in due time. You jus' stick wit dis here Michael character. You be awright. But if'n he start to treat you bad, mess wit yo' mind too much, you jus' come see yo' ole Uncle Clyde. I be right here underneath da bridge." He glanced at Michael, and they both started laughing again.

Just then we heard a loud screech. We turned to look and saw a car desperately trying to skid out of the way of a pedestrian crossing the intersection. The car struck the man, knocking him into the air and across the street. It was painful to watch. He landed on the curb, apparently unconscious. It happened so quickly and slowly at the same time, it didn't seem real.

Michael, Clyde, and I ran to the scene. It was later that I remembered seeing 'Slow Moving' Clyde running gracefully to the man's aid. I'd thought Clyde was nearly crippled. Michael later told me that Clyde chooses to live and act the way he does because that way people generally leave him alone. He also told me that Clyde always says: "Even the government will let an old crippled homeless man be." I'd never thought about a person choosing to live that way. I tried to understand Clyde's position, but the comforts I was used to didn't allow it.

By the time we got to the injured man, he was lying on the ground with his eyes closed. He appeared to be bleeding badly from the right side of his head. The driver of the car was unhurt. He ran over to assist but didn't know what to do. Michael and Clyde stood there for a few seconds looking at the injured man. By that time, more and more people had gathered around, but no one knew what to do.

Michael knelt down and placed the injured man's head in his lap. Clyde knelt down across from him. *Don't touch him, you guys*, I thought. I couldn't tell if the man was breathing or not, but Michael didn't seem to care. He began to sing a soft melody as he gently stroked the man's forehead. Uncle Clyde was sitting there slightly bobbing his head up and down; not nodding to the beat of Michael's tune, just off in his own world. The onlookers, well, they just looked on. They didn't seem bothered by the sight of two homeless men caressing and singing to an injured man. Or maybe they were like me, frozen with disbelief.

Every once in a while, Uncle Clyde would wave his hand over the man's chest as if he was petting the air. It was a gentle motion that almost went unnoticed. Michael kept singing lightly, all the time with a gentle smile on his face.

After a few precious minutes, Michael and Clyde looked at each other. They looked as if they had a plan, but I couldn't tell what their intentions were. The rest of the crowd and I remained silent.

Michael kept his right hand on the injured man's forehead while Clyde placed his right hand on the man's chest. They held hands with their left hands. Michael stopped singing for a moment, and then the man's body twitched. His body jumped, to be more specific.

We heard a loud siren. Michael placed the man's head on the ground. As everyone turned to look at the arriving ambulance, Michael and Clyde stood up and casually made their way through the crowd. Without looking at each other, they walked off in separate directions as if their exit was planned.

As Michael walked past, he motioned for me to follow. He didn't look at me either. I glanced back at the injured man and noticed that he was now sitting up, wiping his eyes. I realized there was no blood coming from his head. I was shocked and confused. Questions immediately formed in my mind. When I turned to ask Michael about it, he was gone.

When I arrived at my car, I found Michael sitting inside. There he told me that the injured man would be all right. I asked him if we needed to pick up Uncle Clyde. He told me that Clyde would be all right too. We could hear the ambulance driving away as I started the car. I was curious about what had happened but waited until we were on the road and the situation was over before I asked any more questions.

"What happened, Michael? I know that you did something. What did you just do?"

"I helped his body reorganize," he answered, leaning his head against the window and closing his eyes. It was the first time I'd ever seen him appear tired.

"What do you mean 'reorganize'?" I asked.

"His body had gone through a tremendous trauma and became disorganized. You see, each part of a person's body can act like an individual entity. Usually they work together, but when something like that happens, all the parts can take off running in different directions. Clyde and I helped bring them back together. That is the best way I can explain it."

"And you did it by singing?"

"Partially."

"What else did you do?" I asked.

Michael sat up and spoke. "Well, have you ever been to a science museum and seen the exhibit that uses sand placed on top of a thin flat metal plate? You take a violin bow and—"

I butted in: "And as you bow the side of the metal plate, the sand forms different geometric shapes depending on the pitch that's being produced."

"Yes," Michael responded. "The sand responds to the different pitches as clay responds to a potter's hands. But with the body, it is not just the pitch that is important; it is also the tone of the sound that helps produce the desired effect."

"Can you explain what you mean by tone?"

"Tone can mean a lot of things. It can pertain to your voice or to color, or to the condition of your muscles. There is a tone control on your television set as well as one on your bass guitar. Photographers and painters as well as athletes talk about tone. But since we have agreed to talk about Music, I will explain it this way."

He adjusted himself in his seat and continued. "Suppose we go dancing at a nightclub. We walk in and the D.J. is playing Music loudly. The sound system sounds great, the dance floor is packed, and the girls are pretty. What would you do?"

"I would find a pretty girl and ask her to dance." I liked the thought of that.

"What would happen if, all of a sudden, the subwoofers blew out and there were no more lows coming out of the speakers? Imagine the sound. What do you think would happen next?"

"The dance floor would clear," I answered, revising my earlier mental picture.

"Precisely! Why?" he asked.

"The subwoofers create the low bass frequency," I responded. "They shake the whole room."

"Yes, and they actually shake your whole body," he added. "With a powerful system you can feel the bass vibrating right through you. When your body starts shaking, it's like you're already dancing just from the sound of the speakers."

"I get it. And if the subs go out, I lose the feeling and don't feel like dancing anymore," I added.

"Even if the girls are pretty?" he asked, smiling at me.

"Right," I chuckled.

"Very good," he said, resting his head against the window again. "You see, tone is a powerful thing. Even though the same Music would be coming out of the speakers, the change in tone would cause everyone in the club to feel differently and therefore act differently. So with this in mind, you should understand that the notes you produce on your bass guitar will have different effects on your listeners depending on the tone that you use. Sometimes tone is the deciding factor that causes a person to listen to you, or not."

"I never thought about tone in that way before," I stated.

"If you want your audience to dance, you should use a certain tone. If you want them to quiet down and listen, another tone may be necessary. If you want them to be healed, an altogether different tone may do the trick. All I did with the man in the street was use tone and pitch to convince his energy to reorganize in a way that would cause his body to heal."

I wanted to understand all of it. "What do you mean by the word 'convince'?" I asked.

"When you are healing someone or something, the choice to become healed, or not, is not completely yours. Don't ever think that it is. You are only in charge of what you are doing. The energy you are trying to heal must agree with what you desire. And on some level, the person or thing being healed must also agree. There are many agreements that must first be made. That is why all attempts to heal do not happen the way one wishes them to."

That information was strange to me. I understood what he was saying, but I had no idea if it was true. All I had to go on was what I'd witnessed. Michael had a way of making anything understandable. Even if I didn't completely understand it the first time around, I knew he would say it again in another way. I sat back and waited.

"The same is true when playing Music," he continued. "Have you ever realized that on some days you seem to have it, and other days, under the same circumstances, playing the same songs, you can't seem to find it? Do you think that it's all up to you, or does Music have a say in the matter? Most of us think that it's only up to us. That would be a mistake."

The thought of "music having a say" was too much for me to grasp at that moment. He spoke about music as if it were real. That made me wonder. Not knowing what to think, I decided to ask another question.

"I noticed that his head had stopped bleeding when you left. Did you do that? And if so, how did you heal him so fast?"

He gave me a typical Michael answer. "Fast? What is 'fast' except a reflection of your personal perspective of time? And what is time except a misrepresentation of now? I tell you this: *All* healing is instant. You are either sick, or you are well. There is no in-between. So the only thing standing in the way of being instantly healed is *time*."

"Wow! I guess you're right," I said, though I knew I would have to spend more time contemplating that statement. "I want to understand. I really do. Can you put it in terms that I might be able to understand right now?"

"Understand this," Michael instructed. "Time and space are the only things that separate one thing from another. Take time and space out of the equation and what is left? Oneness! That's it! But even though one could say that time and space are illusions, they are important. They serve a purpose. Without them we would be unable to observe and experience individuality. The game would be over."

"Do you mean the game of life?" I asked.

"Yes, Life as we know it anyway. You see, when you dream, you are allowed to play by different rules. Dreams allow the sub-conscious to play itself out instantly. Wherever you want to be, there you are. Whatever you want, or don't think you want, there it is all created by you.

"Now *real life*, as most people call it, can be looked at as 'long-form imagination,' a place where things take time. The addition of time and space slows down our reality and believe me that is a blessing. In other words time and space allow us to stop and smell the roses—or get pricked by its thorns. Learn to manipulate these elements and you play a different game altogether. The choice, even if made unconsciously, is always yours."

"Unbelievable," I replied. "And music? How does that fit into this scenario?"

"The same is true in Music," he continued. "There is really only one note. Space and time allow you to experience the different characteristics of that note, making it appear as many different notes. Understanding that will help you make any note fit in at any time. How you see it is always up to you. Think about it; Music and Life would be much different without time and space."

"Okay, I think I'm even more confused now," I told him.

"Look at it this way," he said. "If a person has a cold and breathes on you, are you in danger of catching his cold?"

"Of course," I replied.

"Well then, doesn't it make sense that it should also work the other way around? If I am more healthy than you are sick, shouldn't my healthiness rub off on you? Shouldn't I be able to help make you well?"

"Now that makes sense to me, I guess," I answered, "although I've never heard anyone talk about it before. So that's what you did to the man? You imposed your healthiness on him?"

"Yes, in a sense," Michael answered. "And now you understand how staying healthy can benefit more than just you alone. Because I am healthy, I had a model which I could impose on him. That is one way to help others find health. Think about the word: *healthy*. It's made up of two words: 'heal-thy.' So you can choose to heal-thy self or to heal-thy brother. The choice is yours.

"Like playing an instrument, there are many techniques that can be used. I used tones, healing tones. When we reached that man, Clyde and I listened to see how his body resonated. Only then could we choose which healing tones to produce. Then, like the violin bow at the science exhibit, I used the vibrations of my voice to alter the tones of his body. I needed to reorganize them into a more harmonious state. I didn't need to sing loudly because the vibrations were traveling through my hand and into his head. That produced a direct connection. But the tones have to be accurate in order to produce the desired effect."

"I'm trying to understand, Michael. I really am. What was Clyde doing?"

"Clyde was helping to push and sort of herd the body's vibrations in the right direction. Remember when I said that all the parts of his body were running in different directions? Well, his energies were scattered. Clyde helped to realign them. Once they had decided to regroup, we held hands, said a quick 'thank you,' and were on our way."

"I saw his body jump," I stated.

"The soul will sometimes separate itself from the body in these types of situations to shield the person from extreme pain. Upon reentering, the body will often jump. That's all."

"That's all?" As strange as that experience was, there was a quality to it that seemed to make sense. "This is crazy stuff, but for some reason it all sounds very natural. You guys are way beyond me. Now you're gonna tell me I can do something like that with my bass, right?"

"I don't think I have to tell you. You already know. Music, like everything else, is vibrations. Doctors use lasers to operate. What are lasers but vibrations? Music, in the right hands, can do the same thing. Remember this: The right notes cannot do it alone. The correct tone, as well as dynamics and emotion, must be used. Actually all the elements of Music must be present. These elements are the same as the elements of Life."

The elements of music. The elements of life. I could say the same words but somehow I knew they didn't have the same meaning. He said they were the same elements. Sometimes I felt as if I was able to keep up, but other times I felt utterly confused. This was one of the confusing times. My desire to understand all of it at once caused me to become frustrated. I wanted more answers even though I wasn't sure what the questions were. Michael responded to my confusion with some soothing words.

"You say that you saw us heal an injured man on the street. If you take Clyde, the injured man, and me, and remove the elements of time and space, how many people would there be?"

"One," I answered.

"Remove time and space and tell me how many people were at the scene."

"One," I answered again.

"How many people are there in the world?"

"One."

"How many in the galaxy?"

Again I had to answer, "One."

"And is this one person sick or well?"

"Well, I hope," I answered.

"Then make it so!" With that comment he turned and looked out the window. I offered no response.

While driving, I reflected on the many new ideas Michael had introduced me to in the short time since I'd met him. Many things I'd witnessed him do were impossible, or so I'd thought. I longed to learn how to do every one of them, and he was the perfect one to teach me, or so I thought. Somehow, he seemed to hold the key to unlock hidden parts of my brain, parts that never before existed, or so I thought.

I developed a new sense of respect for him that day. Observing how he and Clyde cared for that injured man allowed me to see another side of him. I knew that Michael was crazy and often acted that way, but watching him pull it all together in a crisis like that was incredible. He conducted himself in a serious and direct manner, not with the questionable and quirky behavior that I was used to.

I remember once hearing him complain about a theory being taught by a highly reputable physics professor at a prestigious university. Michael was outraged, claiming that the professor's teachings were based on theory instead of experience or direct knowledge and therefore should not be taught as truth. Realizing that the professor in question was teaching at a university half a country away, I asked Michael how he knew what was on his curriculum.

"I told you; knowledge is in the air," he answered. "I just need to get that professor to realize it."

Not totally believing in his sincerity, I asked him to call the professor if he had a problem with him.

"Good idea," he responded.

Without hesitation he picked up the phone and dialed. I wondered how he knew the number and whether or not he would repay me for the long distance call. But what perplexed me most was hearing him talk to the physics professor.

Michael spoke in a tone I'd never heard him use. He used words that were bigger than my apartment. I didn't believe he was actually speaking to anyone until, as if reading my thoughts, he asked me to silently listen in. Picking up the other phone, I eavesdropped while he gave the physics professor a physics lesson. I was dumbfounded. I had no idea Michael knew anything about the subject. I couldn't understand a thing he was saying, but the professor seemed to follow along easily, although hesitantly.

I almost laughed out loud when the professor asked Michael how he knew so much about matter. Michael responded that it didn't matter. It was *what* he knew that was important. He told the professor to allow matter to teach him about physics rather than allowing physics to teach him about matter. Then, after showing his students how to do the same, they could have group discussions based on observation, not one-sided lectures based on theory. The conversation ended with the professor apologizing to Michael and promising to modify his lectures and his teaching methods.

Remembering how Michael spoke so fluidly about physics with the professor while also being able to seamlessly blend with a homeless man on the street made me wonder about him and his mysterious knowledge. It was remarkable that he could be equally comfortable dealing with people as diverse as a physics professor, a homeless man, and a wannabe bass player. He'd also just healed an injured man in the middle of a crowd of onlookers by singing to him. I didn't know what to think.

Hearing him speak about tone raised more new questions in my mind. From what I'd heard him say, I could alter someone's body, mind, or attitude, just by altering the tone.

Was it really possible? I thought about how I felt when listening to some of my favorite musicians. I loved their tones even though each one was different, and I realized that my mood often changed whenever I heard them play. Was it their tones that affected me? I was starting to see tone in a much broader way, and I finally understood how it is used to fill up a dance floor. But how could I use it to do other things, more positive things, more mysterious things? That, I would have to explore.

Michael hadn't specified where he wanted to go, so I drove him to my house. I decided to wait until we were inside before I bombarded him with more questions.

Upon our arrival, I found a surprise waiting for me.

Phrasing

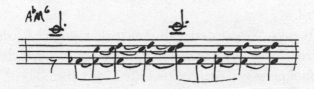

Anything, including physical actions, can be phrased.

When we reached my house, Uncle Clyde was already there. Not outside where most people would be waiting; he was inside sitting in the chair, of course, where Michael's friends seemed to feel right at home.

Don't ask me how he got there before we did. Once we'd left the accident, Michael and I got into the car and drove straight home. As far as I knew, Clyde was still walking away when we left. The fact that he was already inside the house didn't surprise or bother me even though I knew I'd locked the door. I was happy to see him. I hadn't felt comfortable leaving him at the scene. I'd wanted to pick him up, but Michael seemed to know better.

"Hello, Uncle Clyde."

"Howdy do, son." Uncle Clyde seemed relaxed in my

home. He was sitting in the same spot both Michael and Sam had been. *I guess Clyde will be doing the teaching today.*

"I can see that finding the key isn't necessary for you either," I joked.

He looked at Michael and they shared a boyish smile.

"That was amazing what you guys did out there," I commented.

"Thanks. We can't take all the credit, though," Clyde remarked. "Since Life was involved, she deserves some of it."

"So, I guess you decided that life is alive then."

"Oh, we already knew that. We were just trying to figure out how anyone could disagree."

I noticed that Clyde was now talking in what I would call a normal dialect. I wasn't sure whether it was appropriate to comment about it or not, but I decided to anyway.

"Uncle Clyde, I noticed that your voice is different now. Why did you change the way you talk?"

Uncle Clyde looked at Michael before responding. "We change the way we talk according to the situation we are in or the desired effect we want to create. People react certain ways in response to how we act. You understand how the tone of your voice can change the meaning of what you say, right? Well, it can also change the meaning of what you play. I know that Michael already talked to you about that. So understand this: certain vibrations and situations can be created by the words and *phrases* we use. That's why we choose them carefully. Because of how I act, talk, and live, people usually leave me alone. And I's likes ta be left alone."

"Remember," Michael added, "actions, as well as words,

are vibrations, and how we put them together can produce different vibrations, sort of like notes. An individual note sounds one way and produces a certain vibration. A group of notes put together produces different vibrations. A group of chords will produce altogether different vibrations. For example, a group of vibrations can produce a scale. It can be a major, minor, diminished, or any type of scale. These scales produce different sounds and feelings. A longer group of notes, scales, chords, or words strung together is called a phrase. Now a phrase, put together in a particular way, can cause miraculous things to happen."

"The common person relates phrases to words only," Uncle Clyde added. "We musicians go a little further and add notes into the phrase category. Michael and I know that anything, including physical actions, can be phrased, and that is what helps us do what we do. You see, all the elements of Music can be phrased, not just notes. How to use these different elements is what you've been learning."

Once again, it was new information for me. And, once again, only some of it made sense. I knew that certain phrases sounded better than others, but I didn't understand how to actually use phrasing to produce a desired effect. I did understand that all things could be grouped or phrased. At least, I thought I did.

"Listen son, how old are you?" Clyde asked.

"I'm twenty-five."

"Let's see now. That means you've been alive for a little over 9,000 days. If you had a dollar for each day that you've been alive you might not even be able to buy a new car. Think about that. Now let's say that you make it to fifty years old. That's only 18,250 days. Even if you live to be seventy, you're still only about 25,550 days old, not including leap years. A dollar a day and you still can't buy a house. If we were to attach the same value to our days that we do to our money, we might understand how precious little time we have here on this planet."

I'd never thought about that. The old man's ideas were as wild as Michael's, and I was impressed with his rapid-fire addition. I couldn't do that. I wasn't sure where his dialogue was headed, but my mom always told me to respect my elders. Since he wasn't finished, I kept listening.

"Now let's look at how many of these 25,550 days are spent doing nuthin'," Clyde continued. "Let's say that you sleep eight hours a day. That comes out to one day's worth of sleep every three days, a total of 8,516 days. Subtract that from the original 25,550 and you are left with only 17,034 days. That's fewer days than if you live to be fifty. Now add in your early years when most of your big decisions are made for you, the hours spent watching TV, time spent being sick, time spent working a job you didn't like, and days that were just flat out wasted for one reason or another. Now how much time do you think is left? Just a few thousand days, that's all. And that's taking for granted you make it to see your seventieth birthday. That's not much time for you to become who you say you want to be unless yous learn ta use yo' mind."

Clyde pointed to his head and then to me. Scooting to the edge of his seat, he lowered his voice to emphasize his next point.

"Now listen here, son. How much of your precious little

time is spent really becoming who you choose to be? Do you know? Actually all of it is, but you don't know that it's *you* doing the choosing. How much of that time is spent consciously making yo'self better? Not much. We can probably count that time in weeks, or even days.

"If you were to look back over yo' Life, you could find time frames when yo' actions did produce the outcome you were looking for. For example: you spent a few weeks learning how to walk, and you succeeded; you spent a few months learning how to talk, and you succeeded; you've spent years learning how to play the bass guitar, and you have succeeded. *All the things that you've held yo' mind to, you have accomplished, or will accomplish.* You can believe that! And all of these time frames can be viewed as phrases. Normally, when talking about time, we call them phases. Both terms are correct, and even the spelling of the words gives a clue to their relation."

Clyde was putting out so many interesting ideas that I was having a hard time keeping up. I was glad when he finally paused. It would allow me time to digest his words, or so I thought. Michael didn't allow it. He stepped forward taking advantage of Clyde's recess.

"There is only one reason that you ever fail at anything," Michael stated, "and that is because you eventually change your mind. That's it!" Michael raised both hands in the air to stress his point. "Like Clyde told you," he continued, "anything and everything you have ever decided to do, you have succeeded, or will succeed, at doing. It may take you a day, a year, or twelve lifetimes, but if you hold your mind affixed on the idea, it *will* come forth. It has to. That is the law!" He looked over at Clyde, and they nodded at each other in agreement.

They were making bold statements. I'd never thought about those ideas before that day, and at that time, I wasn't sure if I believed them. They both made it appear so simple, too simple, which raised a lot of questions in my mind.

"The only reason I fail is that I change my mind?" Did he mean just me, or was it true for everyone? Was it true at all? And what was this "law" Michael had talked about? The comment about holding an idea for "twelve lifetimes," that was crazy talk as far as I was concerned. I would've liked to have questioned them about it then, but they left me little time to think, let alone raise questions. I suspect they did so on purpose.

It took years before I realized what they were talking about. I eventually thought about all the things I'd ever learned, from tying my shoes to algebra. Well, I never really learned algebra, but whatever I'd decided to learn and continued to learn, I'd eventually succeeded at learning. The things I'd failed at, especially the things I repeatedly failed at, I eventually stopped trying to learn. Michael and Clyde were right. I had simply changed my mind. Even though there were still things I'd not as yet mastered, I couldn't think of a single instance to refute their claim.

Uncle Clyde interrupted my thoughts. "So what I was saying before Michael chimed in is this: your Life is made up of a string of many different phrases. Most of these phrases were put together unconsciously. Now that you realize you only have a matter of days on this planet, it may be wise for you to start living consciously. The choice is always yours." He nodded to let us both know that he was finished.

"Whew!" I sighed. "I never realized that our time here was so short."

"Most people don't, until it is too late," Clyde added.

"Okay, I'm starting to feel a little depressed now. Cheer me up somebody. Let's talk about music again. Can we?"

"Music," Michael stated, "is what we have been talking about all along. Call it Life or call it Music—there is no difference except that most people's musical lifespan is much shorter. And only when the separation disappears for you will Music become a part of who you are.

"You can see how setting up certain phrases in your Life can produce desired results days, years, or decades later. Musical phrases can be set up in the same way. If you are playing a show, what you choose to play at the start of the night can determine how the listener will hear you later in the show. You can use certain musical phrases to 'set up' his ear or his emotions for something you choose to play or do later."

I understood most of what Michael was saying, but I wasn't sure if I fully understood his "setting up the listener" concept. As I was contemplating that idea Uncle Clyde started playing his harmonica. He sounded so good that I wanted to join in with my bass, but I remembered to listen first. What I heard sounded great, but it didn't make me believe that he was the best in the world (as Michael had said), at least not yet.

Clyde started by playing simple and repetitive phrases that were common to harmonica players. I'd heard harmonica players play these types of lines many times before. Realizing that he was playing a blues progression, I finally joined in. Once I started playing, I noticed how *in the pocket* he was. His feel was incredible. Even though he was repeating the same simple phrases over and over, it was starting to sound better and better.

Just as I started to wonder if he was ever going to play anything different, he changed his pattern. He started slowly building upon the phrases he'd set up in the beginning. After a few more choruses he began to solo on his simple blues harp like no one I'd ever heard in the past, playing notes and phrases I never believed could come from that instrument. And then, to my surprise, he took it up another notch. He started playing amazing lines and phrases while humming different ones at the same time. It was so incredible that I wanted to stop and listen, but I didn't. He bobbed his head, rocked his body from side to side, and stomped his feet, adding to the excitement.

After about ten minutes of the most unbelievable harmonica playing I'd ever heard, he went back to the simple phrase he'd started with. For some reason, it sounded better now, much better than before. It sounded and felt like home.

Uncle Clyde was an incredible musician. Then I understood what Michael was talking about. I looked at Michael, and he gave me a reasurring nod. I still couldn't understand why Uncle Clyde chose to live the way he did—a homeless man living under a bridge. He could be making loads of money playing or teaching music. Trying to figure that out by myself was way too puzzling, so I asked him about it.

"Why aren't you out playing gigs, making records, teaching, or something like that? You could make a good living playing harmonica the way you do."

I'm not sure that Clyde ever answered my question. He seemed to have his own agenda when he spoke.

"What did I do?" he asked, placing his harmonica in his breast pocket.

"What do you mean?"

"You just heard me play. What did I do?"

"You played some unbelievable harp," I answered.

"Besides that. What did I do to *you* when I played?"

"To me? I don't know what you mean."

"Think about it," Clyde instructed.

He leaned back in his chair and waited. He was staring at me as if he could see inside me. I thought for a few moments, searching hard for an answer before I finally realized what he was talking about.

"You set me up. Yeah, you set me up! That's what you did. And you did it in a way that I didn't even realize it was happening. First you started with simple phrases, simple repetitive phrases, and you made sure that these phrases were familiar-sounding too. They were sing-able, and you kept playing 'em until I became real familiar with 'em. Then, you changed 'em. At first, I must admit, I didn't think that you were that good, but then your phrasing became jazzier, in a way I never thought I'd hear on a harmonica. Your phrases also changed in length until it seemed like you weren't even

187

breathing. Then, after taking it to the highest level possible, you brought it back to the beginning, bringing me back home again."

Clyde smiled as he commented, "Oh, you think that was my highest level? That was just the highest level I knew you could understand. I could've taken you to another galaxy and left you hangin' way out there to dry if'n I'd wanted to. I took it easy on you, son."

Both he and Michael started laughing, so I joined in too.

"What you didn't notice," Clyde continued, "was that I also phrased the tempo. I started out playing way behind the beat to make you feel laid back. Then, as I started to change it up a bit, I combined rushing the tempo with laying back on it. This caused your body to feel a bit uneasy inside. Then when I played those long, fast jazzy lines, I played on top of the beat. I rushed it just a little. I also left very few spaces, making it sound like I wasn't breathing. I had you holding your breath, whether you realized it or not. At the end, I quickly came back to my original phrase, laying back behind the beat again. That made you exhale and relax, like you were in a familiar place. And even though you didn't, you wanted to put your bass down and start applauding. I know you did. Works every time." He spread his hands and leaned forward in his chair, taking a bow.

He was right. I had felt the urge to applaud.

"I've never known that much thought to be put into a solo on the spot, especially on the harmonica," I commented, adding a little humor of my own.

"I know what you mean. 'Thought' is usually reserved for you bass players. Ain't that right?" Clyde answered.

"Touché," I replied.

"You ever hear about someone breaking a glass with a high pitched note?" Clyde asked. He picked up my empty orange juice glass that was still sitting on the table from Sam's visit.

"Yes I have. I've never seen it done, but I've heard about it," I answered.

"That ain't nuthin' but vibrations. And if they can shatter a glass, imagine what they can do to your body. Now, I can do the same thing by setting up phrases. The proper use of phrases allows me to gradually change your mind and body. Changing it all at once can cause your head to explode jus' like that glass. All I do is set up groups of vibrations to produce the same or similar effects. But instead of one powerful vibration, I can use a group of vibrations. It can be done in the course of a solo, or it can be done over the course of a whole night. You know, it can be done over the course of a few days if you want to. You can 'set up' yo' listeners to hear or feel things in a particular way later on in the night, or later on in their Life. That's all Michael's been doing to you. He's been settin' you up one phrase at a time. Actually, you's been doing it to yo'self for years too; you jus' didn't knows it. You's been settin' yo'self up for dis event fo' a long time now." He reverted to his old way of talking for effect I guess.

"You mentioned that before," I said, "something about me getting ready for this time, or something like that. What are you talking about?"

Uncle Clyde looked at Michael as if to get permission to speak. He slowly stood up and walked over to me. He stood so close that our noses almost touched. I could feel the warmth of his breath as he prepared himself. Whenever Michael stood this close to me, I knew that he was going to say something important. Clyde's brown eyes pierced my soul as he looked at me. I widened my stance and readied myself for his words. He spoke in a gentle whisper, but with a serious tone.

"You're at a special time in your Life, son. You might say that you're ending one phrase and starting another. What direction you play this phrase in is completely up to you and don't ever think that it's not. This is important! It's time for you to take control of your Life and for you to accept that it is *you* who's in control. You understand?"

He took a step back and continued. "You see, mos' musicians play a bunch of notes and hopes dat a good phrase comes out. Dat's awright, but it ain't da best way. If you keep yo' mind on da feel, da shape, or da purpose of da phrase, all da right notes will come out on dey own. Dis is how we talk, ain't it? We don't pay no attention to every word unless we has to. It's da feeling, da meaning dat's on our mind. You can get all messed up if'n you tries to pay attention to every lil' note. You can do it like dat if'n you wants to—ain't nuthin' wrong with it—but it don't make much sense to me." He lowered his head, shaking it side to side.

"So you're in control of the phrases, but you release your control of the individual notes?" I asked.

"But I can control 'em notes too if'n I want to, or if'n I don't," he answered. Taking his seat again, he pulled his harmonica out of his pocket and used it to gesture. "I use control and no control at da same time. 'Cause see, if'n yo' phrases keeps coming out wrong, you may needs to go down to da level of da individual notes to see what da problem is. You understand? If you jus' think about how yous talk, it'll all make sense. Add dis system to da way you play and da way you live yo' Life, and you'll be awright."

All of a sudden, when I finally felt as though I was starting to comprehend what was being said, a thought from an earlier conversation entered my mind, pushing all understanding aside.

"But wait a minute!" I shouted. "Michael, just a few minutes ago you were telling me something about 'time' being my perspective. Then, Clyde, you were talking about how 'precious little time' we have on this planet. Now, that seems like a contradiction to me. I'm confused, again."

"That's 'cause you can't hardly believe anything that Clyde says," Michael snickered.

"What? Why not?" I asked.

"Because he'll probably tell you something wrong, something exactly the opposite of what I say," Michael answered.

"Well then who should I believe?"

"Don't listen to dat fool. Listen to me," Uncle Clyde mocked with a smile on his face. "I only tells da trufe, da whole trufe, and nuthin' buts da trufe."

"No! You should only believe what I say!" scoffed Michael.

"Don't believe nuffin' he say!" Clyde shouted.

"Wait a minute! You guys are really confusing me!" I shouted in return. "I don't know who to believe or what to think anymore."

"Perfect!" Michael stated, nodding his head at me.

"Perfect?" I answered. They were feeding my frustration. "How is that perfect?"

"You don't need to believe none of us," Clyde answered in a gentle tone. "You need to listen to us. That's all."

"Well then, who *do* I believe?"

"Well then, who *do* you believe?" They almost answered in unison.

They knew I hated that type of answer, so I just glared at both of them.

"Who makes your decisions for you?" Clyde asked.

"I do!"

"Then who do you believe?" Michael asked again.

Michael was irritating me and he knew it. Glancing back and forth between the two of them was compounding the effect. I stood there for a moment trying to compose myself before I answered. Looking back on it, I see what they were doing. Their antics helped me form my own conclusion.

"I guess I should believe myself," I answered.

"That's right, son," Uncle Clyde confirmed.

Michael patted me on the shoulder and nodded. "Very good. I can tell you have more to say about that. What is it?"

Michael kept his hand on my shoulder which helped me relax. I felt inspired, so I spoke. "I should listen to all that you or anyone else has to say. Then I make up my own mind. *I* choose what I want to believe. And if I'm having trouble figuring out what the truth is, what *my* truth is, I ask questions, listen, and let experience talk to me." I had it and I knew it.

"Bingo!" Michael exclaimed.

"You ain't half as bad as Michael said you was," Clyde added, laughing.

Michael stepped over and stood between Clyde and me. It was his turn to stand as close to me as he could. His green eyes twinkled as he spoke.

"If you believe what we say all the time, you may never come to your own realization. And your own realization is the only realization there is. If we tell you different things, you will be forced to decide for yourself. And your own decisions are the only decisions you should ever make. But when you can't decide, you will have to rely on experience. If you have no experience to draw from, trust your feelings. That is always best because *your* feelings are the only ones that will always speak the truth. If you are still unsure, test all the theories to see which one works. Often times you will find that more than one will work. But that still leaves you with a decision to make. Your decisions are best made by you and no one else."

Clyde stood up and pushed Michael aside. He waved his hands at him saying, "The kid just said that, Michael, and with less words too. You were always the wordy type. Let me talk to the boy."

Uncle Clyde walked over to me and stood with his nose to mine again, to emphasize the importance of what he was about to say. It still surprised me to see him move with such grace after the slow, aged way he had moved when I first met him.

"You just needs to listen to all of it, son," Clyde continued. "Keep yo' mind open to all the information. That'll help you make the best decisions. One bad decision today can cause yous to end up way off course later on down the line. You understand, son?"

"I do, Uncle Clyde," I answered.

"Good! Don't forget it then." He nodded and turned toward his seat.

I liked Uncle Clyde. His mannerisms were very different from Michael's. Although Michael was a born clown, it was Clyde who made me want to smile every time he spoke. Clyde's demeanor reminded me of a Stradivarius violin. The older it gets, the sweeter the sound. And what he had to say was music to my ears.

"Why do they call you Uncle Clyde anyway?" I asked him.

He slowly took his seat before replying. "Because I's related to everybody. You see, Brother Clyde or Father Clyde sound a bit too religious to me. Plus dey don't quite have da same ring to 'em as Uncle Clyde do. Both Cousin Clyde and Grandpa Clyde sound pretty cool, but I's older den yo' cousin and younger den yo' grandpa. Now dat's all I's gonna say about dat. I's tired of talkin'. Michael, listen here; go ova' dere and pick up dat guitar. Kid, you grab da bass.

Let's make some Music."

Space/Rest

Life is a lot like Music.
You've gotta put some rest in there.

"Zero," she said.

"What?"

"Zero."

"What about it?"

"It is a mysterious number, my child."

"So?"

"What does it mean to you?"

"It means nothing to me!"

"Exactly! It means 'nothing,' but it also means 'ze most.'"

A few days had gone by since I'd last seen Michael. The time we'd spent with Uncle Clyde was an eye-opening experience, and our all-night jam had left me wanting more. Listening to those two guys play together was like hearing two brilliant minds speak on any subject they chose. Sometimes I could understand what they were saying but most of the time I just sat there in awe, enjoying their interactions.

I spent the next few days practicing my bass, waiting for either one of them to return and answer the questions I still had. Knowing that Michael would often show up unexpectedly, I hadn't left the house for fear of missing him. On the third day I awoke feeling tired, bored, and lonely. I picked up my bass but immediately knew I was in no mood to practice. Trying to escape my troubled thoughts, as well as get some fresh air, I placed the bass on the floor, put on my shoes, and hopped in the car.

Driving has always been good for my mind. It seems to put it in a good space. That day, however, I didn't want to be gone for too long so I cut my drive short and headed to the nearest bookstore to see if I could find anything else by Tom Brown, Jr.

I was hoping to make a quick stop but my plans were thwarted by a most intriguing character. As I walked through the entrance of the store, a woman rivaling Michael's peculiar appearance grabbed my arm. I knew my day was about to get very interesting.

"Zero, I say," she repeated, her long purple nails gripping my arm. "It means ze most, no?"

"What are you talking about? No! It doesn't mean the most," I answered, looking down on her. "It means nothing! The first number is the number one! Before that, you have zero, which is nothing!" I don't know why I continued to indulge her by answering. It seemed a futile exercise.

"You are correct, but you are also wrong," she replied, looking up at me through her glasses and offering a curious smile.

I shook my head. The conversation had just begun, and I was already frustrated. I didn't have time for her. I was in a hurry. All I wanted to do was make a quick stop in the bookstore and get back home. I hoped that Michael would be dropping by, and I didn't want to risk missing him. Well, life had another plan for me that morning and Michael would have to wait because just inside the entrance of the store, I found myself engaging in a strange conversation with a very strange lady about, strangely enough, nothing.

Just inside the front door of the bookstore was a small table with one chair. The table was covered with a purple fabric, and on it sat a crystal ball surrounded by a circle of cards that were either blank or facing down. A single candle stood burning in the corner.

The Amazing Isis: Seer of Past, Future, and Now! *Also, Free Gift-Wrapping* the sign on her table read. Like I said, she was strange. She was also short, very short. I guess she stood about four and a half feet tall (in heels). Standing there in front of her, I could imagine what Dorothy from *The Wizard of Oz* must've felt like towering above the Munchkins. I thought about clicking my heels three times but knew that it wouldn't get me home any quicker.

Isis spoke with a heavy accent (Russian, I guessed) which required me to listen closely to every word. The way she looked up at me through her black-rimmed glasses reminded me of a cross between a schoolgirl and my grandmother. I could envision myself carrying her books and at the same time see her scolding me for not doing my chores.

Her clothing was as odd as Michael's. She wore a long flowing purple dress wrapped in beads and bells that rang and clanked when she moved. Covering her shoulder-length brown hair was a non-matching purple bonnet laced with flowers. It was the old fashioned type of hat that seemed to come right out of a Southern Baptist church. Her feet were partially hidden by the hem of her dress. Though I couldn't see them, I could tell by the sound that she was wearing ankle bracelets.

Perhaps the funniest part about her appearance was her beauty mark. Just to the left and underneath her bottom lip was a big black mole. There were three hairs sticking out from it, all thick enough that one could easily see them. Her mole bounced around whenever she spoke, reminding me of the musical bouncy ball that's used on television to help people follow along with the words of a song. I hoped it would help me too because I was sure having trouble on my own.

As soon as I'd walked through the door, Isis stepped in front of me. When I tried to walk around her, she grabbed my arm to stop me from passing. I guess that she needed someone to talk to and I was the lucky victim.

I was used to these types of conversations with Michael and I knew that grin, but standing there with that short peculiar lady put me in unfamiliar territory once again. And although a little irritated, I was eager to find out where the conversation was heading.

"Okay, please explain," I said.

"Yes! Let us have a look." She walked around the table and took her seat behind the crystal ball, placing both hands on the table. "You are correct zat one is ze number coming after zero, but is one ze first number?"

"Okay, zero is the first number, I'll give you that, but it still means 'nothing.'"

"What happens, zen, if you put 'nothing' after ze number one?" She turned over a card with the number one written on it and slid it toward me.

"Nothing happens; you still have the number one," I answered.

"Oh no you don't."

"What do you mean?"

She turned over another card, this one with a zero on it, and placed it to the right of the one card. "Put a zero after ze number one and you have ten," she stated.

"Well . . ." I stammered, trying to think of something clever to say. She sat back in her chair allowing me time to ponder the thought. I was already tired of her smile.

She had me though. She was right. I'd never thought about it until then. The number zero, when placed after any other number, is like multiplying that number by ten. *Hmm . . . zero is more than nothing.*

"Hmm . . . yes, it is," she affirmed.

I gave her a surprised look. She broadened her smile, causing her mole to rise. Her mannerisms reminded me of Michael's. The things Michael had to say were always so interesting that his victorious smile no longer bothered me, but seeing her with the same look was a little bit scary.

I knew that I could never win an argument with Michael, but it never stopped me from trying. He always seemed amused by my efforts, and was forever baiting me with tidbits of information. Like a carrot dangling in front of a donkey, I guess it kept me moving forward. Right then I felt that she was doing the same thing.

"So you see," she continued, "what zis shows us is zat zero is a powerful number. But actually, it is more zan a number. It is a principle. It is ze principle zat allows all ze other numbers to exist and expand. Zero is like ze base, ze foundation. Without it, zere would be no other numbers."

"Wait a minute," I uttered. I wasn't sure what I'd just heard her say. Was she talking about a base or a bass? She gave me no time to ask.

"So I propose zis thought to you: Ze number zero is actually superior to all ze other numbers, and here's why. Ze numbers one through nine always represent something. Zey can never represent nothing. Zero gets to represent something *and* nothing. Like ze bass, it usually goes unnoticed, but it can be on ze bottom and on ze top. It is zis fact zat makes it complete."

I didn't totally understand it, but it was interesting. I still wasn't sure if she was talking about a bass or a base. I started to ask, but she put a finger to her lips and then to her ear indicating that I should shut up and listen.

There was only one chair at her table, and she was sitting in it. Moving closer to her, I stood opposite and above her as she spoke. I felt like a giant looking down as she flipped her cards and occasionally looked up at me. Although I towered over her, I knew that I was the underdog in the situation. Her outlook on zero was enough to make me forget why I'd come to the store in the first place. Somehow, I sensed, there was a correlation to music although I hadn't yet figured out what it was.

Isis showed me other interesting things about numbers, like how the numbers one and nine are related. The number one, when added to itself, will always 'increase' by one (ascending scale) while the number nine, when added to itself, will 'decrease' by one (descending scale). For example:

$1 + 1 = 2$
$1 + 1 + 1 = 3$
$1 + 1 + 1 + 1 = 4$
$1 + 1 + 1 + 1 + 1 = 5$, etc.

Nine plus nine, repeated, produces numbers with descending values in the ones column.

$9 + 9 = 18$, (EIGHTeen),
$9 + 9 + 9 = 27$, (twenty-SEVEN),
$9 + 9 + 9 + 9 = 36$, (thirty-SIX),
$9 + 9 + 9 + 9 + 9 = 45$, (forty-FIVE), etc.

In multiplication, she related zero to the number nine because both always revert back to themselves. Any number multiplied by zero always equals zero, and any number multiplied by nine always results in a number that adds up to nine. I already knew that the number zero would revert back to itself, but I never realized how nine does the same thing. For example:

$1 \times 9 = 9$
$2 \times 9 = 18$, $(1 + 8 = 9)$
$3 \times 9 = 27$, $(2 + 7 = 9)$
$4 \times 9 = 36$, $(3 + 6 = 9)$, and so on.

She showed me more eye-opening things about numbers that day such as how each depended on others to exist. She told me that each number, while displaying its own unique characteristics, also possessed qualities similar to those of its brothers and sisters. She was able to show the similarities between numbers and people too. I never figured out which numbers were male and which were female, but she seemed to think that there was a difference.

A lot of her information was interesting and different, but what intrigued me most was listening to her talk about zero. She kept relating it to the bass, or maybe it was the base. I still couldn't tell. I just kept listening.

"Like ze members of a band, all ze numbers have unique and important responsibilities," she continued. "Zero is ze yin yang number. It represents opposites, something and nothing, fullness and emptiness, big and little, power and weakness, bottom and top. It is not a coincidence zat its shape is round. A circle is ze shape of space. It has no beginning and no end. Many masterful things possess zis shape. It is a holy shape. It is also ze shape zat all things eventually revert back to. Even a straight line, if continued long enough, will in due course make a circle."

It is also ze shape of your mole. It was about all I could focus on, the way it bounced around. She looked up at me with a frown but didn't comment. *Even with Isis, I'll have to remember to watch what I'm thinking.*

"Like a black hole," she continued, "a vortex zat sucks in on one side and spits out on ze other; zero has ze ability to show us both sides of something."

It was a bit unnerving how much she reminded me of Michael. It wasn't just her mannerisms or her outlandish appearance; what she said and the way she said it seemed peculiarly familiar. Somehow, I knew that all the number stuff would circle back around and relate itself to music.

I didn't quite understand all she talked about or why she was talking to me about it, but she held my attention. I'd never looked at zero that way. For that matter, I hadn't looked at any number that way. Her erratic movements let me know that she was excited just talking about it. Peering into her crystal ball, she continued, this time in a softer, more mysterious tone.

"Zero is like space, you see. It is ze base of all things, and from within zis space all power comes forth. A scientist looks close enough at an atom and what does he find? Space!" Her arms flailed when she said that word.

I thought back to my high school science class, trying to remember anything I'd learned about atoms. I remembered my science teacher saying something about an atom consisting of a nucleus, protons, neutrons, and maybe something else, but that it was mostly filled with space. Or maybe he was talking about molecules. I couldn't remember. That left me with no way to dispute Isis's information, so I didn't try. I knew that there was no way I could manipulate her. Trying to manipulate four bass strings had already caused me years of struggle.

She quickly looked up at me and responded. "Strings! You want to talk about string theory?"

"Oh no," I replied, realizing once again that my thoughts might not be mine alone.

"Okay zen, we will stick with numbers and Music."

"So you *were* talking about music," I commented, my eyes opening wide. Once again she pressed her finger to her lips.

"Listen," she said. "Ze same way a luthier looks inside a violin. What does he find? Space! Look inside ze bass, and what do you find? More space! But what comes out of zis space? Music, you see.

"Split an atom (full of space) in ze wrong way, and BANG! You can be certain of what will happen." She stood up and thrust her arms in the air. "But zere is no need to do zat," she continued, taking her seat again. "If ze scientist could also look inside your mind, what would he find? He would find nothing but space. Ze same space found inside of zat powerful little atom can also be found inside your mind. Zis should give you an idea of ze power your mind possesses. It is in ze 'nothingness' of your mind zat infinite power resides. So ze next time you say zat you have 'nothing to do,' you should recognize ze potential power in zat statement."

She looked up with a smile and winked at me, then lowered her head and continued gazing into her crystal ball.

"Are you saying that my mind is more powerful than an atom bomb?" I asked.

She looked at me and tilted her head in a way that only a loving mother could do. "Oh my child, an atom bomb is designed to do one thing and one thing only, but your mind is designed to be unlimited. From ze 'nothingness' of your mind, all things of zis world and other worlds are born."

"Other worlds?" I had no idea what she was talking about. She was on a roll that I couldn't stop, so I filed it away in my mental vault and just kept following the bouncing ball.

"Anything can be found within your mind," Isis told me. "Zat is where all Music lives, in ze space. Emptiness is ze key. Think of something and zen surround it with emptiness, one big zero. Your intention is enough to do ze rest. Your mind does ze shaping, yes, but your mind creates nothing, no more zan your bass creates Music. So no more trying, only space. Trying to make something happen is like trying to walk a straight line when ze policeman asks you to."

I remembered Michael using the same "policeman" example. I didn't know if it was a coincidence, or if Isis and Michael had somehow coordinated this chance meeting. I started to ask her about it, but she continued talking.

"Zat is a mistake many people make when trying to enter into ze world of conscious creating. You are creating everything anyway, so when you try too hard, you push it away. Again, ze keys to everything can be found in space."

I was following some of what she was saying, but not all of it. Like talking to Michael, it was hard keeping up with the countless bits of information coming from Isis, but I tried my best. And also like Michael, she had a way of staying slightly ahead of me. Not wanting to miss anything, I struggled to keep up. I guess they could both pull me further along that way.

Isis talked for a while longer relating numbers to everything she could think of. I forgot about the time and willingly listened. When she was finished, I wandered around the bookstore in a daze trying to make sense out of anything she'd said.

Once I'd remembered what it was that I'd originally come for, I found the book, paid for it, and walked back to Isis's table. Even though I was buying the book for myself, something caused me to go back over to her again. Maybe it was to get my purchase gift-wrapped. Maybe I somehow knew she had more to say. Maybe it was I who had more to say, or maybe it was the way her long purple fingernails dug into my arm as I tried to sneak past. Whatever it was didn't matter to her. She made sure that I listened. Holding me with one hand, she grabbed her chair with the other so she could stand on it. Now looking me in the eye, she continued her torture . . . I mean lecture.

"Listen my son, what I tell to you." Her nails were piercing my flesh, forcing me to pay close attention. "You don't understand me now, what I tell to you, but one day, one day, it will all make sense. Listen to ze numbers my child, all of zem, and understand ze importance of zero. Only zen will you truly understand ze power of space.

"Whatever you hold in your mind, don't let disrupting thoughts get in ze way. Place your thoughts in ze middle of a big fat zero. Like ze nucleus of an atom, zis is powerful. When you learn to place yourself in ze center, surrounding yourself with zis power, zis space . . . zen, whatever you choose is certain."

She paused, looking up to her right as if she was remembering or maybe receiving a thought. Then tightening her grip on my arm, she returned her gaze to me and continued speaking, in a near whisper this time.

"Listen! Before you can fully understand the notes, dear boy, you must first understand the space you will place them in. Space can be seen as the birthplace of all things. That is why all things are eventually attracted back to it. This is the principle of 'zero.' Pay attention to what I am telling you! Your understanding of this will allow you to pack your Music with an immeasurable amount of power, the power to change the world and the power for the world to change you. But remember, you are responsible. It is now time for you to go." She winked at me as she released my arm and stepped down from the chair.

"My music?" I almost shouted. "What does all this number stuff have to do with music? Hey wait a minute. How did you know that I play music?"

Her arms flailed through the air once again as she answered my question, in her own way. "My dear boy, you are blind, are you? Did you not read ze sign on ze table? I see everything. Everything! Now, give me zat book!"

Wrapping books was definitely not her forte. I wondered how she got the job. Ripping paper and tape, she tossed the book from side to side, knocking her cards all over the floor.

I started to offer assistance but before I could speak, she did.

"You stay wrapped up in ze present, and leave ze wrapping of presents to me."

I didn't want to leave it to her. She was clever with her words, but not with my book. She appeared to be mutilating it. *The poor lady could really use some help.* She looked up at me and frowned once again.

As she continued wrapping, thoughts and questions about her flooded my mind. *Did she know Michael? Where had she come from? Where did she come up with that crazy number system? How did she know I played the bass? Or did she know? Did she accost other customers this way? Who at this store was crazy enough to hire her? Who convinced her she could wrap books? And, once again, did she know Michael?*

I was also curious about the way her eyes seemed to change. I don't remember if they ever changed color, but they definitely changed in some way. Although Sam was only eleven, I realized that he had it too. I hadn't connected with Isis's eyes until she'd stood on the chair. It was then that I knew for sure she was talking about music. The only people I'd ever met with eyes like that were all connected to Michael. It may not make sense, but it was as though music spoke through their eyes.

Our chance meeting seemed too much of a coincidence. Had Michael arranged it? He must have. That thought had been eating at me the whole time I was in the store. I finally got up the courage to ask Isis directly.

"Do you know Michael?"

Her answer was immediate. "I've known Mr. Jackson

since he was just a baby. I was ze chief advisor at ze Neverland Ranch for eight years, but Mr. Jordan came to me only once. He had no idea what to do with Bird and Magic, but since I am an expert on both birds and magic, I quickly set him straight. Mr. Douglas was a local Shakespearean actor before I found him. Now you see where he is today. And Mr. Angelo, I knew him before he converted to ze one-name format. He would still be painting stick figures if it weren't for me. Oh, I'm sorry. Which Michael were you referring to, my child?"

"Okay, okay, thank you very much for your time," I mumbled. She acted like what she said was true, but I knew differently. I felt I could get a more honest answer from Michael himself. Grabbing my book, I ran out the door. Her voice echoed in the distance as I hurried to my car.

"What about ze tip?"

I was almost home when I realized that Isis's accent was practically non-existent when she spoke to me about music. Was it her, or was it me that made the change? I wasn't sure.

The thought was washed away when I got out of the car and heard the most amazing music coming from inside my house. I knew that it was Michael playing the guitar. I was happy that he was there. I stood outside listening for a full two minutes before his voice interrupted my bliss.

"Are you just gonna stand there, or are you searching for the key?"

I opened the door to see him sitting in his usual chair with his usual grin. It was the same smile I'd just seen on Isis's face as I was running out of the store. Setting down the guitar, Michael answered the question that was on my mind. (At least, I think he answered it.)

"Music *is* numbers, you know."

"So you *do* know Isis," I said.

"Oh, you mean ze lady zat works at ze bookstore mutilating all ze books?" he mused.

I had to laugh. "Did you arrange our meeting at the store?"

"Isis is strange," he remarked.

He'd ignored my question, but I didn't mention it. As strange as Michael was, it was odd hearing him refer to someone else that way.

"But she does know her numbers," he continued.

Although I'd missed much of what Isis had said, I knew her information was somehow relevant. Wanting to get a better idea of how numbers relate to music, I asked Michael about it.

"They relate in every way," he answered.

"What do you mean?"

"Have you ever heard of iambic pentameter?"

"No," I replied. "What is that?"

"It is a rhythmic structure that is sometimes used in writing. Shakespeare used it. So have many others. It's numbers, that's all. How about haiku? Have you heard of that?"

"I think so, but I don't really know what that is either."

"Don't worry about it. Try this one. In Music, you do understand how one relates to eight, don't you?"

Finally, a question I knew the answer to! "The number one, *Do*, is the root. If you count the notes of a major scale, *Do—Re—Mi—Fa—So—La—Ti—Do,* one and eight are the same note an octave apart."

"Okay then, what note would the number zero represent?" he asked.

I had to think for a while, but then the answer hit me. "I've never thought about it before, but the answer is obvious. Zero has to represent space, no notes at all. If zero makes all the other numbers possible, space must make all the other notes possible." I inhaled as a broad smile formed on my face.

"Isis would be proud," Michael remarked. "Now taking it past the elementary, you can apply this concept to notes, rhythm, technique, dynamics, space—all the elements of Music, but let's just stay with intervals for a moment."

Notes and rhythms were one thing, but how I was supposed to relate numbers to the other elements was a mystery to me. I was lost again, and Michael had barely begun.

"Fourths are related to fifths," he said. "Do you know how? No? Because *C* to *G* is a fifth if you are moving up, but a fourth if you are moving down. Going from *G* to *C* works just the opposite. Now, a major third is related to a minor sixth. For example: *C* to *E* is a major third while *E* to *C* is a flat sixth, but a minor third is related to a major sixth. Hmm! *C* to *D* is a whole step while *D* to *C* is a minor seventh. Is *C* one half step or six steps away from *B*? Who knows? Let's look at a tritone. You can get from *C* to *F sharp* by playing three whole steps or two minor thirds. Going from *C* to *F sharp* is the same distance away as going from *F*

211

sharp to *C*. That, to me, is a perfect interval, but *C* to *G* is called a *perfect* fifth. Interesting. It's nothing but numbers! Understand?"

"Absolutely not!" I answered proudly.

"Good. I like an honest answer," said Michael. "All knowledge is not meant to be put in the microwave."

"I think I get that," I stated.

"Many people will study hard trying to understand all that information at once, not realizing that it probably wouldn't make them play any better. Knowledge is not meant to be gathered all at once. Allow Isis's information to simmer. All that she told you will make sense in due time. I'm more interested in what else she had to say about 'space.' Did she tell you about the birds and the bees?"

"She did say something about birds and magic," I answered.

"Perfect! Isis is in tune today," he said to himself, clasping his hands together. "What she told you had to do more with your mind than anything else. I told you that Music is played with the mind. She gave you some simple clues how to use your mind to its full potential."

"You call that simple?" I asked.

"Her message is simple, yes. You allowed her words and numbers to confuse you. Once you learn to do what she suggests and understand the power and value of space, then you will really understand the power of Music and the mind."

"I don't know how anyone could understand her broken English."

"That is because you focused on her words instead of her

message. If you would just empty your mind and allow the meaning to enter in, it wouldn't matter what language she spoke. You would understand it just like Music. The same process can be used to communicate with anyone or anything, including animals."

"What?"

He couldn't be serious, could he? What happened next was unbelievable. I don't expect you to believe it because I barely do, and I was there, but here is exactly how I remember it.

Michael told me to go outside and look up. So I did.

"What am I looking for?" I asked from the front yard.

"In twelve seconds a male red shouldered hawk will fly almost directly above your head," he answered.

I didn't understand how he could possibly know that because he was still inside sitting in his chair. But once again, he was correct.

"Wow! How did you know that? Did you hear it coming?" I asked running back inside.

"Yes and no," he answered.

"What do you mean?"

"I didn't have to hear the hawk. I listened to the other birds."

"Cool, what did they say?" I was excited to hear his answer. I expected a mystical, magical reply that was going to blow my mind. What he told me was so simple that, well, it blew my mind.

"The birds said nothing, or 'zero,' as Isis might say."

"What do you mean?" I asked again.

"When a bird of prey is on the hunt, most smaller birds know it. So, trying their best not to become the hawk's meal, they do their best to become invisible. Many of the other birds will hide and become silent. When I heard the birds stop singing, I knew there was a threat approaching through the air."

"How'd you know the threat was in the air and not on the ground?" I asked.

"Birds scream at a threat on the ground because they know they are safe in the trees. If the threat is another bird, the trees may not provide them with adequate cover, so the birds become silent, dive into the bushes, or both."

To let him know that I understood, I said it in my own way. "What you are saying, then, is that you listened to the silence the birds created."

"Exactly! Very well stated," he replied. "And how the silence moved across the landscape allowed me to estimate the speed of the hawk's approach."

That was amazing. It was so simple that I couldn't believe I'd never noticed it before. In the past, I had noticed when the birds were singing, but it never occurred to me to pay attention to when the birds *weren't* singing. How he knew it was a red shouldered hawk and not a red tailed hawk or some other bird was still a mystery to me.

"Once you pay attention to the silence, or the 'zero' factor, you will learn to decipher the different types of silence," Michael said. "Remember, zero is related to other numbers. That means that zero or silence can change. Your understanding of that will let you know what type of threat is approaching."

Well, I didn't understand. Different types of silence? And how did he seem to always know what I was thinking? *Oh well, a little at a time.*

"Come, watch this," he said with a smile.

We walked outside and Michael began making a series of short, high-pitched squeals. He repeated the sounds intermittently until something amazing happened. The red shouldered hawk circled above us getting lower and lower. After a few passes, he landed in the tree across the street from my yard.

"He might do it," Michael whispered.

The hawk then flew down to a lower branch. There was no way I could get myself to believe what was about to happen. It was just impossible. As I had that thought, I could imagine Michael telling me that anything is possible.

"Anything is possible," Michael said with a wink of his eye. "Now quiet your mind, remain still, remain calm, and allow the silence to speak louder than your thoughts."

How I was supposed to do that was a mystery to me, but I tried anyway. To my amazement, the hawk swooped down from the tree and headed straight toward us. The closer it got, the bigger it looked. I glanced at Michael to see if he was as nervous as I was. He stood there firmly and slowly raised his arm.

The red shouldered hawk—the wild, untamed bird, the huge bird of prey—perched on his arm. It was unbelievable and beautiful at the same time. The bird, with his broad brown breast and his sharp hooked beak, lowered his head and allowed Michael to scratch the back of his neck.

"All animals like to be petted," he stated. "Birds like to be scratched on the back of their necks. It's a hard place for them to reach."

He asked me to stick out my arm, and again, to my amazement, the hawk jumped onto it. I was surprised at how scary it felt. The bird seemed to notice my apprehension and started to flap wildly until Michael reached over and resumed scratching his neck. After a short while the hawk also allowed me to scratch his neck. It was incredible to see the big bird lower its head in order to be petted, instead of lowering his head to bite my fingers off.

"Animals respond to your feelings," Michael stated. "You need to get your thoughts out of the way so that your true feelings can speak."

"How do I do that?" I asked.

"How do you do that?

"Meditation, I guess." That was the first thing that came to mind, so I went with it. "I've heard of people using it to clear their minds but I've never really understood how to do it. Can you teach me how to meditate?"

"I will show you what to do," he answered. "You can teach yourself."

When would I ever learn?

We said good-bye to our hawk friend and watched him fly away. When we got back inside Michael closed the window shades and instructed me to sit comfortably in a chair.

"Clear your mind, listen to my voice, and pay attention to how you feel."

He was sitting on the floor behind me and speaking in a soft, soothing voice. He also spoke more slowly than usual. I was still excited about what I'd just witnessed and couldn't stop thinking about it.

"Excitement is a true feeling," he stated, "and true feelings have power. You can use this power if you know how. The excitement you feel causes your body to tingle. Pay attention to that feeling and allow it to encompass your whole body. Surround yourself with the tingle."

I sat there for a few minutes trying to do what he asked. The more I tried, the harder it became. I could hold on to the tingle only when I didn't try.

"This is an exercise in mind and body control," Michael said. "Don't think about it. Allow it to happen. This is the time to use 'not concentrating.' Use intent, not focus, to get the body to do what you ask of it. Clear your mind and use your feelings."

I tried for a few more minutes until I got frustrated and opened my eyes.

"I don't get it," I said. "I'm trying real hard to hold onto the feeling, but it seems as if the harder I try, the more the feeling slips away."

"What you've just said may hold the key to your solution," he told me. "Don't try real *hard*, try real *easy*. Treat it like a game, no pressure. If it doesn't work, big deal. Like holding water in your hand, it takes a gentle process."

I closed my eyes and took a deep breath. *Try easy,* I told myself. I chuckled at the idea. After what seemed like only a half minute, I was feeling it. I could feel the tingle in my whole body. Michael allowed me to sit with the feeling for a while. Once I did, he told me to make the feeling smaller in size, but not in intensity. He asked me to envision the tingle as a concentrated ball of energy and then place it into the center of my chest. Once I'd succeeded at that and was able to hold it there for a while, he asked me to move the ball around to different parts of my body. He said that any feeling could be moved around that way.

"Doing this could be very healing or very damaging," Michael said. "It depends on the intent."

Every time I focused on the fact that I was actually doing it, the feeling would start to go away.

"Let it go," he instructed.

Once I was able to relax and "let it go," the feeling came back. It responded in an unexpected way. The more I tried to hold onto it, the faster it would run away. The more I released it, the more it stuck around. I wasn't sure, but it seemed like all I needed to do was use intent to direct the tingle. Physical effort seemed to have the opposite effect. Once I had the tingle where I wanted it, I moved it all around my body until Michael asked me to let it fill my whole body once again.

After that was accomplished, he went on. "You are surrounding the tingle with your body. Now allow it to surround you."

If anyone could hear what he was asking me to do. I tried not to think about it.

I imagined myself inside the tingle. I could see it all around me as if I was in the middle of a golden orange-ish cocoon made of light. Somehow he seemed to know when I'd succeeded at one phase before guiding me on to the next.

"Now that it is outside your body," he continued, "you can either walk away from it, leaving it there, or you can send it somewhere else. Right now I want you to send the tingle over to me."

I heard him walk across the room but I didn't open my eyes.

How am I supposed to do that? I thought to myself (or so I thought).

"Come on!" Michael responded. "A child would not ask how. Just allow it to happen. Use your intent. Play like a child."

I didn't know what to do, so I improvised. I inhaled and envisioned my tingle as a golden light surrounding my body. I mentally stepped away from it so that I could see it as its own entity. Upon my exhale, I blew it over toward Michael. I watched it travel slowly across the room. I almost laughed out loud because it looked like a big zero. As soon as I imagined it hitting him, he responded.

"Very good! Very, very good! First try. I'm shocked and a little bit jealous. I completely missed the hawk the first time I sent my intent bubble over to him. He had to change tree limbs just to catch it."

My eyes opened on their own. Feeling a bit dazed, I shook my head as I listened to him, not knowing whether or not he was patronizing me. Whichever it was, it was working. I was amazed and elated about what I'd just accomplished.

After a moment of celebration, Michael walked up to me and looked me straight in the eyes. I couldn't tell what color they were, but in the darkness of the room his eyes seemed to glow.

"Now," he continued, "this is real serious stuff. You can treat it like a game when you are just beginning, but even then, your intent must be pure. Once you are confident with your abilities, the power increases. At that time, how you use it has a tremendous effect on all Life everywhere. Right now, you can treat it like a game, but know that it is not one."

He gave me a few seconds to think about what he'd said before he leaned even closer to me and continued. I could feel his eyes searching my soul, looking to see if his words were taking root.

"You have no idea of the extent of this power," he told me. "It can be used to heal yourself, someone else, or it can be used to . . ."

He looked across the room. I followed his gaze. There was a flower sitting in a vase on the kitchen table. One ray of sunlight snuck in through the window shade, illuminating a few of the petals. To my astonishment, as I was looking at it, the flower wilted. It literally fell over. I almost did the same. My mouth fell open in disbelief. I looked back at Michael. He was smiling. He winked at me and then glanced back at the flower. I looked again, and to my surprise, the flower was alive and perfectly healthy. I looked back at Michael not knowing what to think.

"You believe in that stuff?" he asked. His Cheshire-cat grin was in full effect.

I didn't know what to believe. I stood there with my mouth wide open, glancing back and forth between him and the plant. He turned and walked toward the front door. As he opened it, he looked back at me, making a final statement.

"Meet me at the Grapevine Café at ten. Tonight we will turn all of it into Music."

With a gentle pull of the door he was gone and I was left standing in the dark, contemplating yet again what was real and what was not.

The Grapevine Café is a small nightclub in Nashville located on Elliston Place. Elliston Place is a short street full of thriving businesses during the day and a very active nightlife scene. There are about three or four different bars and nightclubs on the small street.

The café only holds about one hundred and fifty people, but the large window just off the stage provides anyone standing outside a great view of the band. On that particular night, the street was packed with people trying to see and hear through the window. I didn't know if Michael had arrived yet, and because of the long line of people, I didn't think I would be able to get in to see if he was already inside.

As I approached the club I noticed someone in the crowd pointing at something. I turned to look and saw a strange sight. There was a man coming up the street wearing a black cape with blue lining, held together at the neck by a silver brooch. An American flag was wrapped around his head, and believe it or not, he was riding a skateboard.

As he approached, I thought about sneaking away so that no one would know that the guy was with me. From inside the door I heard someone shout, "Michael, your table is ready. They're waiting for you."

I ran up to meet him just as he entered the club. "He's with me," Michael shouted as we made our way through the crowded entrance. The look on the faces of the people trying to get in made me glad that I was with him even if he was wearing a cape.

The band was already playing. They sounded amazing. It wasn't until we reached our table that I realized Sam was playing bass.

"I didn't know they let 'em in so young," I joked.

"There is no other player in town who can play like Sam, including you," Michael replied.

It hurt, but it was true. I knew most of the players in town, and no one had a feel like Sam. He never sacrificed the groove in order to play a 'lick' and he always played with a smile on his face, as if he actually enjoyed it. That was impressive. (Do I need to remind you that Sam was only eleven?)

"Tonight is a special occasion," Michael remarked. "These guys don't play together that often. All the band members are at the top of their field, but it is the drummer who I want you to pay attention to tonight. There is no drummer in the world who can regulate the groove the way he does. He is also a master of space. Notice how he uses it to make what he *does* play stand out."

"What's his name?" I asked.

"Not important, just listen," he answered.

Regulate the groove. That was another new concept. I didn't know what it meant, but I was eager to find out.

We listened to the band jam for about forty-five minutes before I realized that the drummer had not taken a solo at all. He barely played any fills, and often left space at the end of phrases rather than fill them up with licks. The groove, I realized, was stronger and more consistent because of it. I could tell that the drummer had chops, but the fact that he wasn't showing them off was impressive. *Maybe that's what Michael meant. I would love to play with that drummer.*

Just then, the guitar player started speaking into the microphone.

"Ladies and Gentlemen, I want to introduce to you a man, the baddest man in all the land. They call me 'the teacher,' but I'm gonna introduce to you the man that taught me all I know, plus some things I don't know, not to mention a few things I shouldn't know. Fresh off of his tour to Never Never Land, two stars to the right, the one and only, never lonely, bad to the bonely—Michael!"

The keyboardist played a fanfare as Michael jumped up onto the table, pulled his cape over the lower half of his face, and bowed down on one knee. He then quickly stood up, holding his cape wide open with both hands as if he were doing his best Batman impersonation. He was quite a spectacle.

The crowd didn't know what to think, and neither did I (although I secretly thought the cape was cool). He jumped down from the table grabbing my hand, and quickly walked to the stage, dragging me along with him. There was no time for me to think.

"What do you wanna do, Michael?" the guitarist asked.

"I want to sing 'Mustang Sally' in *C*," Michael answered. "My friend here wants to play with your drummer. He claims to be a bass player."

I could see Sam laughing as he took off his bass and handed it to me. It was too late for me to claim that I didn't know the strange caped man, so I took the instrument and strapped it on.

As I stood there feeling the stares of the audience, a surge of nervousness and insecurity swept over me. I didn't know what to do. I'd played that song hundreds of times before, but for some reason, that night, I was at a loss for notes.

Michael looked back at me. I was already sweating. How was I going to measure up to the little kid that had been playing all night? I looked at Sam. He flashed a reassuring smile.

Oh, yeah, smile, I remembered.

With four clicks of the drum sticks and no more time to think, the song began, *sans* bass. I was so wrapped up in my anxiety that I forgot to come in. Michael quickly came to my rescue.

"Hold on, hold on! I'm about to drive this thing, but I forgot to fasten my seatbelt." As he pantomimed sitting in a car and fastening his belt, he turned around and winked at me. "Just make it groove," he whispered.

We got off to a good start. I'd never heard Michael sing before. He was incredible. He was a cross between Otis Redding, James Brown, and Bob Dylan, if such a thing were possible. Between running through the audience, dancing, and doing the splits, his pitch never seemed to falter. He also made it a point to perform for the people looking in through the window. How he maneuvered his way around the small stage without breaking something or hurting himself was even more amazing.

After singing a few verses and choruses, Michael pointed at the guitarist, who proceeded to play the most amazing guitar solo I'd ever heard. His guitar screamed and squealed in ways that made the instrument seem alive.

Once he was done, the sax player took his turn. Much of his solo was accomplished while playing two saxophones at once. The keyboard player used a device that had a plastic tube attached. He held the end of the tube in his mouth which made his keyboard sound like it was speaking words. It was incredible. I'd never witnessed a group of musicians who possessed that much ability.

The solos were passed around to each musician until I noticed that it was now being passed to me. I was so wrapped up in each of the previous solos that I'd neglected to realize it would eventually be my turn. That actually was to my advantage. If I'd been thinking about a solo, I would've spent the whole song being nervous rather than enjoying myself. But now, my nerves were like a bomb about to go off. I could feel them taking over my whole body. Michael looked at me and took a deep breath. I took the hint and did the same.

Everyone stopped playing except for the drummer and me. I've always hated when that happens. All the other solo-ists get to play with the whole band while the bass player has to play with just the drummer. Well, he wasn't "just a drum-mer." Playing with that guy was like lounging on a large plush sofa.

He was sitting behind the drums looking at me, waiting for me to begin. The groove that he laid down was so solid that it actually calmed me down a bit more, but I still didn't know what to play. All I knew was that I was *not* gonna let an eleven-year-old kid get the best of me, at least not in public. I decided to play it all.

I started my solo with a flash, and the more I played, the more insecure I felt. I closed my eyes and tried to get deeper into the music. Everyone else had taken a lengthy solo, so I de-cided to take my time, saying everything I wanted to say. I used all of my techniques and played every note that I knew.

Opening my eyes, I looked at Sam; he was smiling. Re-membering my lesson with him, I started smiling too. It worked a little. Michael was sitting next to him, whispering some-thing into his ear. I knew they were talking about me. Trying not to let it get to me, I closed my eyes again.

That night, even though I was nervous, I played what I thought was one of my better solos. When I finished, the crowd went wild. I felt so good that I couldn't keep myself from smiling. I tried to appear cool by stepping back and lean-ing against the speaker as if it was an everyday occurrence. I looked at the drummer, waiting to see how he was going to follow me.

Looking calm and cool, he just sat there chewing bubble gum with his head bobbing up and down. He didn't appear concerned with me at all. The groove he was laying down was the heaviest and most solid I'd ever heard. Basically, he kept doing what he'd been doing the whole song.

After about eight measures or so of intense grooving, he stopped playing. He just completely stopped. His head was still bobbing up and down with the groove. I looked at Michael and Sam. Their heads, along with every head in the audience, were bobbing up and down.

I was amazed that even though no one was playing the drums—or any other instruments, for that matter—the groove was still there. The whole room could feel it. It was as solid as it'd been all along. The fact that he'd laid down such a strong groove for so long allowed us all to continue feeling it.

After about four measures, he hit the splash cymbal one time. He then proceeded to sit there, in silence, bobbing his head and chewing his gum for another four measures. After that, he was done. That was his solo. He simply returned to playing the same groove he'd been playing before. It was remarkable.

I was blown away. It was the most amazing solo I could remember hearing, ever! Even the thought of approaching a solo that way was pure genius. His solo said more than the rest of ours combined, and he did it by saying nothing. I could hear Isis's voice ringing in my head repeating the number zero over and over. I was finally starting to understand that principle a little bit more.

The drummer had created space in a way that allowed the few beats he did play a chance to really be heard. He did it in a way that forced us, the listeners, to hear them. And we heard them completely. It allowed us to appreciate each drumbeat wholly. I was getting it, and *it* excited me. *This drummer is a genius.* I knew I had more to learn about using space, and I looked forward to finishing the song so I could talk to Michael about it.

When it was over we shook hands with the band members and I gladly handed the bass back to Sam. I was eager to get off the stage so I could ask Michael what had happened. I wanted to know exactly how the drummer had done what he'd done. I understood it on a surface level, but I knew there was something deeper going on, something I was missing.

Back at the table, Michael told me to keep listening. He said that I could ask the drummer myself after the gig was over, so that's exactly what I did.

At the end of the night, after all the equipment was packed away, Michael and I sat with the drummer and talked for awhile. Sam couldn't stick around because he had school the next morning. There were many things I wanted to know about space and how to use it. I asked the drummer if he would talk about it for a few minutes before he left.

"Michael should be talking instead of me," he answered. "He showed me the way into this world. I just explored it and learned to use it in my own way."

"Well you sure are doing a great job," I told him. "What you did tonight was unbelievable."

"Thank you," was his modest response.

"Can you help me understand space the way that you do?" I asked.

"Start by first understanding *rests*," he replied. "Rest is related to space, but not as broad. Your solo tonight was really good, but you rushed at the end of almost every phrase. You were not in the right space. You played as if you had something to prove. That caused you to rush. You were so anxious to play the next group of notes that you neglected to play the rests. You didn't give the notes their full Life, their full amount of air. In simpler terms, you played the notes but not the rests. If you don't play the rests, give them the same attention that you give the notes, you'll rush, simple as that."

"I never thought about that," I commented.

"I could tell. Most people don't," he replied.

He was being completely frank with me, but I didn't mind.

"When we first take lessons as kids," he continued, "we learn how to read Music and we learn what rests are, but we rarely learn how to really play them. And we are never taught how to *use* them. We know how to use notes to produce desired results, but we are never taught how to use rests that way. If we pay attention to the rests and really learn how to use them, we find that they can speak louder and deeper than notes."

"Louder and deeper than notes? What does that mean?" I asked.

"If you're performing for a noisy audience, and you want them to stop talking and start listening to you, what do you do?" he asked.

"Play louder I guess."

"Wouldn't that just make them talk louder?" he asked.

"I guess it would. Maybe I should play quieter to make them listen."

"Right, or stop playing altogether. Think about it. A baby will sleep through any noise that's going on as long as it is constant, but if the noise stops, the baby will wake up. Why? Because he's been deeply touched by loud silence." He made a light tapping gesture on the table.

"Oh yeah," I said, not realizing how I could have forgotten. "I saw Michael stop a guy from talking just by using dynamics, and that guy was all the way across the room."

The drummer smiled at Michael and remarked, "Still doing tricks, huh Michael?"

"I always did love a good parlor trick," Michael answered with his usual smile.

"Michael could stop a guy in Cincinnati from talking if he wanted to," the drummer added before continuing. "Listen to all the background noise that's going on right now."

He sat back, so I did the same. I could hear the bartenders and waitresses as they chatted and closed up for the evening. There was music playing over the sound system that I hadn't paid attention to until that moment, as well as the sounds of cars and people outside. I hadn't realized it before, but all of the noises were causing us to speak louder.

"What would happen," the drummer asked, "if all the noises suddenly stopped?"

I thought about it for a moment before he answered for me.

"You would become 'dead' silent. Your ears would perk up and you would listen intently in the direction the silence came from. You'd be searching for a cause and your aware- ness would reach out to the next available sound that stood out. Now what you have to do is learn how to create the same effect. When you're playing to an inattentive audience, you and your bandmates are the background noise. Something must change before you can cause the audience to listen. They may decide on their own to start listening, or you can decide for them. You can make them listen without their even knowing it. The best way to do that is through dynam- ics, or even better, through space. Create silence and let the next sound that speaks to them be your bass. If done well, they'll listen to you for the rest of the night. That's all I did for my solo."

"You used space and you really used it well," I remarked.

He pointed a skinny index finger at me and responded in a serious tone. "Right, and as you noticed, no one said a word. They were sitting on the edge of their seats waiting to hear what I was gonna do next. The space came from my direction, so they all looked at me. I had them in the palm of my hand. At that point I could've done anything with 'em, but I decided to let 'em off easy. How did I do it? By playing *nothing!*" He sat back, smiled, and continued chew- ing his gum.

That was remarkable to me. I couldn't wait to learn how to use space in that way. Even though everything he said made complete sense, I didn't know where to start. He sat up quickly and replied to my thoughts.

"Start with rest," he stated. "Learn how to make a rest speak louder than a note. Play a musical line and then start leaving notes out, putting the emphasis on the rest. You should end up playing more rests than notes. Have you talked to him about projecting his intentions?" he asked, looking at Michael.

"Yes," Michael answered.

The drummer scooted his chair closer to mine. Leaning over, he put his mouth to my ear and whispered. "Create space in the appropriate way, then fill the space with a solid emotion. You won't have to project it nowhere. The space you created will draw the listener right into it. And then . . ." He scooted his chair away and began to stand up. "Aw man, that's the good stuff. Learn how to make that work, and you are on your way."

With that comment, he was on his way. As he turned to leave, I thanked him for the lesson and told him that I hoped to play with him again.

"Oh you will," he replied as if he knew something I didn't. "Life is a lot like Music. You've gotta put some rest in there. And right now, I've gotta go get mine. Later! I'll catch you another time."

Before he walked out the door, he turned to take one last glance at a beautiful waitress walking by. "Just admiring God's work," he remarked. I watched in silence as he made his way to his car.

Michael sat there smiling the whole time. He seemed to enjoy watching my mind get blown by someone other than himself.

"He's incredible," I stated.

"He is also credible," Michael replied.

"I think he enjoyed playing with my mind as much as you do."

"Most people *work* with their minds when *playing* with them can be much more effective," he responded.

"Did you teach him all that stuff?" I asked.

"What I showed him is not as important as whether you learned anything tonight, or not. Did you learn?"

"But of course."

"Good, because we must leave now.

We have a meeting with a frog."

Listening

We think that Music stops at the ears.
That is a mistake. Vibrations can be felt in all places and
at all times, even with the eyes.

We drove for a few miles to a place called Radnor Lake. "Radnor," as it's called by the locals, is one of Tennessee's most beautiful state parks. Located near the Green Hills section of Nashville, Radnor is home to an abundant variety of wildflowers, birds, reptiles, and mammals. The eighty-five acre lake attracts naturalists, bird watchers, and hikers from all around. Its trails, which traverse some of Tennessee's highest hills, along with the lake, make it a popular place to visit all year round. It's a favorite site of mine, and a place I'd been to many times before but only during the day. I'd never been there after dark.

We parked at a nearby store and walked down a darkened

street which led to the park entrance. It must have been cloudy because no moon or stars were visible. That, coupled with the fact that there were no streetlights, made the walk seem as dark as if we'd had our eyes closed. The distant sounds of the forest added to the eeriness of the morning. Michael walked slowly in silence, often pausing as if he were listening for something.

"This way," he said.

He led me to a bench on the far end of the lake. "*Listen,*" he whispered, as he quietly sat down. We sat in silence for a time, listening to the chorus of crickets, frogs, and other insects that filled the air. The sounds were mesmerizing, and lulled me into a trance until Michael spoke.

"Pay attention to how the animals are listening to each other," he instructed.

I hadn't noticed it before, but the animals did seem to be listening to each other. It sounded like the different species were taking turns singing. When the animals did speak on top of each other, they did so in a different register. It was like listening to a well-orchestrated masterpiece.

I was enjoying the music until an airplane flew overhead, causing all the animals to become silent. After the sound of the plane faded, the animals attempted to restart their chorus. It took awhile for them to get back in sync, as if each musician wasn't quite sure when to come back in.

"There is a species of frog," Michael stated, "that uses their unison chorus for survival. When they speak together, they sound like a much larger animal. Unnatural sounds, like that airplane, break up their unity, and when they try to join back in, one by one, they are picked off and eaten by predators. Because of that, some species of frogs are becoming extinct. It goes unnoticed by most people. We have forgotten, as a species, how to listen."

I'd never thought about the possibility of noise pollution leading to the extinction of animals. I knew how awful certain noises made me feel, so it was not too farfetched for me to believe that these noises could severely affect other animals too.

I sat in a melancholy trance thinking about it. That is until Michael started making low guttural sounds. I didn't know what he was trying to do. He kept it up for about fifteen minutes, taking short pauses and turning his head as if to listen in all directions.

All of a sudden I felt something land on my left leg. Then, it jumped to my right leg. It startled me. Inside my body, I was screaming. Outside, I was frozen and silent. I would've knocked it into the water if Michael hadn't picked it up first. I tried to focus my eyes in the dark. I couldn't tell what it was until I heard it make the same sound Michael had been making. It was a frog, a rather large frog. Michael turned the frog upside down and started rubbing its belly.

"All animals like to be petted," he said. "This is Betty; she is a friend of mine. Her brother Jeremiah died recently."

"Jeremiah was a bullfrog?" I asked.

"Yes, he was a good friend of mine."

I started to laugh but then realized that he'd said that Jeremiah had died. Just in case he was serious, I acted sad.

"How did he die?"

"Pollution," Michael replied. "This area cannot sustain the number of frogs that it once could."

"What do you mean? I come here all the time. This lake is well taken care of. The rangers make sure that nothing is dumped into it, and—"

"Noise pollution," he replied, interrupting me, "or you can call it 'vibration pollution.' Either way, it is caused mostly by the airplanes and the nearby construction. The Friends of Radnor Lake Foundation has tried for years to get the air traffic rerouted so that the planes don't fly directly over the park. They have tried but have not succeeded.

"Besides adding noise, the planes actually change the vibration of the park. That is not good for the animals or the visitors. Environmentalists know that the planes aren't good, but they do not fully understand why."

"Did Betty tell you that?" I asked, feigning seriousness.

"No, I could sense it. That is why I come here almost every night and sing to the animals. It helps reset the vibrations. The frogs seem to enjoy it the most."

"You sing to them?" I asked, no longer hiding my disbelief. "And you're trying to get me to believe that they actually listen?"

"I am not trying to get you to believe anything. I am just telling you what I do."

"I don't believe you. You're a remarkable man and everything; I'll give you that much. I'll even go so far as to say that I believe you're crazy enough to come here every night and sing to frogs, but you can't expect me to believe that they actually listen to you."

"Oh, they listen all right," he stated, "better than most humans do. Most humans can't listen past their limited intelligence. The more they think they know, the less they honestly hear. Humans only hear what they want to hear. Play a record for a musician, and before he can listen to it, he has to know who it is. And once he knows, he decides what it sounds like before he ever hears it, solely based on what he thinks he knows about the performer. What difference does it make who it is? What does it sound like and how does it make you feel? That is what is important.

"You could learn a thing or two from these animals; they know how to listen. Some of them don't even have ears. They can't hear at all, but they can feel. So with my voice and my whole being I create healing vibrations that combat the damaging vibrations in the air. The animals allow these vibrations to penetrate their whole bodies, the vibrations acting somewhat like vitamins. That is the best way to listen. Allow your whole body to pick up the vibrations, using the whole body as an eardrum."

"I'll have to work on *listening* like that," I *note*d, trying to calm myself down. Michael spoke in a *tone* that seemed to match the peaceful place we were in. I, on the other hand, was speaking through *emotion* alone which made it hard to *articulate* my true feelings. Also, the *dynamic* of my voice was way too loud for the quiet *space* we were in, causing my *rhythm* to differ from that of the woods. Maybe a different *technique* would help. Taking a deep breath, I tried to relax before I spoke my next *phrase*. (Although slow, I was learning.)

"That's an interesting thought," I said, proud of my composure.

"Yes, but not a foreign one."

"But you're still pulling my leg, right? The animals don't really listen to you, do they?"

"You know that plants respond to Music, don't you?" he asked.

"Yes, I've heard about that before."

"Do plants have ears?"

"Well no, I guess not."

"Music, like all things, is vibration; that is all. Because we humans can hear Music with our ears, we get stuck on the idea that that's all there is to it. Most of us wouldn't even consider the thought of seeing Music, or of hearing a flower. What we hear, we do not see, and what we see, we do not hear. We think that Music stops at the ears. That is a mistake. Vibrations can be felt in all places and at all times, even with the eyes. Music can be seen if your awareness is broad enough."

Years earlier, while living in Virginia, I'd played a few shows at a school for the deaf and blind. It always surprised me to watch the deaf kids dance. They could really feel the music. Sometimes we would aim our speakers at the floor to help them feel the music even more. Some of the blind kids even claimed to be able to see the music. I knew that they were responding to the vibrations of our music, but I don't think that I'd thought about it since then.

Although I couldn't imagine seeing music or hearing a flower, what Michael was telling me made a lot of sense, but I didn't like it. I wasn't going to continue letting him suck me in with his sense-making nonsense. He was talking about singing to frogs! Now, that's crazy talk in my book. Feeling my composure backslide, I started to respond but he beat me to the punch.

"Vibrations," he continued, "are penetrating. Like ripples in the water, they bounce off you *and* they go right through you. An important thing to remember is that vibrations never stop vibrating. Think about that. Vibrations may change, but they never stop. That means that we should pay attention to the vibrations we're putting out there."

I wasn't buying it. At least I wasn't allowing myself to buy it, and I was ready to let Michael know it. "Do you charge the animals admission?" I smirked.

"They pay me in their own way," he answered.

"Stop it, Michael! Just stop it! I've heard enough! You bring me out here at—I don't even know what time it is—and spoon-feed me this nonsense! Do you really expect me to—"

I was enjoying creating my own noise pollution when, all of a sudden, I was stopped mid-sentence by a gentle sound. Michael started singing. There were no words, but the most beautiful sounds filled the air. It didn't even sound like it was coming from his mouth. The music was just in the air. I don't have the words to explain what I was hearing. I wish I did. It was angelic. It was . . . well, angelic is the best I can do.

I closed my eyes and let the music envelop me. It was easy to do. It was the first time I'd ever felt music with my whole body. I thought I'd done it before when I heard music that made me get up and dance, but even then, I was only hearing through my ears. At that moment in the woods I was hearing with my whole body, and the music was causing my whole body to tingle. It was a pleasant feeling.

I remembered my earlier lessons dealing with the tingle. I allowed the feeling to permeate my whole being. It felt so wonderful that I wanted to share it. Focusing on the tingle, I allowed it to travel outside my body. I pushed it out as before, but this time I expanded with it, keeping myself attached to it. (It's hard to explain, but I know what I did.)

After a few moments, I felt something wet and cold touch my hand. I opened my eyes and saw a deer standing right in front of me, her nose touching my open palm. Even though I should've been shocked, the feeling was natural and wonderful. I reached out and touched her on the head just to make sure she was real.

I wonder if I'll be able do this again while listening to ordinary music? I pondered.

"Already on to the next experience, I see."

I didn't know where those words were coming from. It felt as if someone was sending their thoughts to me. Then I realized that they seemed to be coming from the deer. I wasn't sure, but as soon as I looked her in the eyes, more words entered my mind.

"All experiences as well as all Music are ordinary. It is up to you to add the 'extra' quality that makes something 'extraordinary.' But like most humans, you risk missing much of the present experience by putting part of yourself in future or past experiences. I highly recommend you spend this moment in the 'now' so that you and the experience can share with each other all that you have to offer."

Her voice was tender and sweet. I'd never been given advice by a deer, so I decided to take it. I closed my eyes again, allowing myself to be fully in the moment.

It felt bizarre being in such a trance while at the same time being so aware. Taking hold of my awareness, I expanded myself even more until I could sense the plants and trees. I got the feeling that they too were listening to the music. I wondered if my aura could get poison ivy. A strange thought, I know, but it went along with the strange experience I was having.

After relishing the music for a while, I opened my eyes and thought it was daytime. That was my first impression because everything was so bright, but then I noticed that the light I saw was a glow. I could see a bright glow surrounding everything, and I was part of it.

I looked at Michael. He was still sitting there with his eyes closed, singing. I could see the music coming from him. It appeared to be mostly emanating from his mouth, but I noticed that it was also coming from his whole body while at the same time entering his whole body. The music was connected to everything and everything was connected to the music, including me. I could see vibrations bouncing off and passing through everything, allowing me to know that all things were alive and connected. I knew where all the animals were. I didn't have to look; I just knew. I've never felt that way before or since. It's hard to put into words, but I felt like I cared so much about all things that I *didn't* care.

I closed my eyes and sat inside the music. I listened to all the sounds around me and noticed how they fit in. Like different instruments in a band, each sound served a purpose. Each animal made a sound that somehow supported the other sounds while leaving enough space for all to participate. The music sounded and felt so wonderful. I knew that the best thing I could offer was silence. So I sat quietly.

As I sat there listening, the orchestra grew stronger. It seemed as if more and more animals and insects were participating. I may have been the only animal in the forest not making a sound, but I knew that I was not the only animal listening. All the animals had to be listening in order to make a collective sound as beautiful as what I was experiencing.

More than ever, I understood the power of listening, just listening. I wondered what music would be like if musicians listened like that?

"Only through the power of listening can you truly know anything."

I didn't know where the thought had come from. It felt as if it came from the music, as if the music were speaking directly to me. At that moment I understood the connection between listening and feeling. I knew that they were the key to understanding everything, especially music. I'd been calling myself a musician for years, but at that moment, sitting in the woods, I was sure that the animals knew more about music than I did.

For a while, I'd forgotten that the core of the music was coming from Michael. Even though his voice clearly provided the baseline of the sound, it was in no way more important than any other voice.

Months later while playing with a band, I thought about my experience at the lake. I was able to use it to remind myself how to listen and fit in with other musicians. My newfound listening skill was one most other musicians neglected. It wasn't that they couldn't listen as well as I could; they just didn't. I noticed that most musicians seemed to reserve their ears for themselves rather than open up their ears to the rest of the band. I found that when I listened to the other musicians more than I listened to myself, I played better. I realize that listening is a choice. The same is true in conversation. When I listen to other people more than to myself, I know how to respond and support them in a better way. It also helps me know when to remain quiet.

Listening with my whole body became a huge benefit at my gigs. The few times I've tried to explain this concept to someone, it proved to be too much of a struggle. Most people can't understand. They approach it as a hypothetical concept, not as a reality. I will have to bring my musician friends into the woods and let them figure it out themselves, I guess.

At the lake, I could feel the presence of all the animals around me. I opened my eyes again and to my surprise, there were about fifty animals of all sizes, not counting the frogs and other small rodents sitting or standing around us. There were deer, coyotes, foxes, bobcats, rabbits, raccoons, opossums, squirrels, beavers, birds, bats, snakes, otters, minks, mice, and more, all co-existing. Some of them were in the trees and some were in the water.

Michael sang for a few more minutes before slowly fading into silence. Soon after, most of the other animals also became quiet while the insects continued their chorus. I sat there in awe, realizing I might never hear anything like it again.

Michael reached over and grabbed a snake that was curled up asleep in my lap. I hadn't noticed it was there. I was so shocked at the sight of all of the other animals that I didn't have time to be afraid of the snake that was now crawling down Michael's arm to the ground.

As the animals calmly went their separate ways, Betty hopped up and again perched on my left leg. Thinking about the snake, I commented, "You almost joined your brother." I reached down and took my turn petting her belly. She seemed to enjoy it.

We sat there for awhile as Michael walked around petting the remaining animals. They came up to him wanting to get closer to the vibrations I could still see emanating from his body. It made me understand the effect some pop stars have on their fans. Do the fans just want to touch them, or do they unconsciously want to connect with their vibrations?

The whole experience seemed surreal. But it *was* real: real vibrations, real energy, real music, and I could feel it! I could see it! I could hear it!

"Now," Michael whispered, "that is how you listen to Music."

I don't know how much time had passed, but by the time we reached the car the sun was almost up. I sat in the driver's seat with my head against the steering wheel.

"What was that, Michael?"

"Don't try. You can't fit it into words."

We drove home in silence.

The Dream?

In all your musical years, when have you ever
truthfully said 'Thank You' to your bass guitar?

I was sitting there "practicing" on my couch. The next thing I remember, I was walking down a crowded street pushing a shopping cart. I don't recall whether it was day or night. I don't even recall being able to see myself, but I know that I was dressed in rags as if I were a bag lady collecting my prize possessions and pushing them around in a cart.

The main difference was this: I was not collecting physical things. I was collecting thoughts. I could hear people's thoughts, and because there were so many, I could not keep up. I couldn't process them, so I carried them in my overflowing cart.

All the people on the street made fun of me and called me names. The thoughts they projected were even worse. They didn't know I could hear them.

247

I thought about all the so called "crazy" people I'd ever seen walking the streets. Maybe they weren't all crazy. Maybe their minds were just open, too open for their own good. Maybe they just didn't know how to process all the information they were receiving.

At that moment, I made a vow not only to change my views about "crazy" people but to listen to them as well. It was amazing to think about the possibilities, of all that could be learned. The possibility of being able to help them was also interesting to me. Maybe I could somehow help them gain control of the information overload.

It was that thought that caused me to realize I was living a duality. I was simultaneously in two different places. I was the bag lady pushing the cart of thoughts, and I was also somewhere else, watching and thinking about it all.

I tried to see if I could get a handle on some of the thoughts that were coming in. Could I help that person (me) control and maybe organize some of the thoughts that were overwhelming me?

I tried to focus on some of the thoughts. The energy in my head and in the cart was swirling, blending together. It was a very confusing mix of information, but there was one force that seemed to be prevailing. I can't explain what it looked like or how I could distinguish it from the others, but I could feel that particular energy was different. I felt it was beckoning to me, so I reached out and tried to grab it. It grabbed me instead. It was a gentle tug to which I immediately surrendered.

I found myself in another place or, more accurately, another space. I can't exactly call it a room because there were no walls, floor, or ceiling. Colors enveloped me and, looking back on it, I realize the colors were constantly changing. I was surrounded by an energy that I somehow sensed was alive. So I decided to speak to it.

"Who are you?"

"I am Music," she responded.

Her voice was sweet, the type that you could melt right into. I don't know why I attached a female gender to it. Maybe it was because of the gentle nature I felt emanating from her.

"Music?" I replied. "I never realized you were really alive."

"I know. You have chosen not to realize it, and that is why your musical Life has never been alive. It is also why mine is fading."

"What do you mean by that?"

"Your approach toward me has been as if I am not real, like I'm a *dream*. You feel that I do not exist until you create me. And even then you feel I am a creation that is separate from you. Most musicians in your time feel as you do. Because of that, I am dying and in need of your help."

I could tell that she was not well, but I hadn't focused on that thought because I hadn't realized Music was alive until then. I could tell there was a difference in the way my new friends spoke about Music. Now I knew why. Music *is* alive and real, but how could she be sick? And why was she asking for my help?

"How can I help you?" I asked.

"When you were young you weren't afraid to dream, and it was those dreams that gave birth to your reality. You knew that I was alive and inside you. You could feel our union and would express it anytime and any way you chose. As you grew older you yearned to know more about me, but through lessons and books you abandoned your own experience for someone else's. The more you learned, the less you felt. The more you opened your eyes, the less you dreamed. The more you practiced, the less you played, and soon you forgot about me. There is no one to blame for this. Your parents and your teachers did what they thought was best for you, but it was that way of learning that diminished a lot of your natural gifts."

"What were my natural gifts?"

"*Knowing* has always been one of your best attributes, but it is one that you are now afraid to use. You do not trust yourself the way you once did. When you were a child, you knew what you knew and didn't question what you knew. There was no need for others' justification or approval. Your experience, coupled with what you felt, was your truth.

"If you felt me inside you, you would sing, play, or dance. You did not need an outside reason for doing it, you did not need instructions on how to do it, you did not even need an instrument. And you surely didn't care what anyone else thought if he or she saw or heard you doing it. It was beautiful. Everyone who was near you would be pulled into our world and, for a little while, they too would feel their connection with me. They would feel the realness of Music."

I could remember doing that as a child. I would get a feeling and, without thinking, just let it out. I'd start singing at the top of my lungs or, sometimes, quietly to myself. I'd dance to a tune playing in my head or to the one floating through the trees. My parents always said that I'd drum on everything I could and that I'd make instruments out of anything that was around. I don't know when or how I'd lost the gift, but Music was right; I *had* lost it.

"How can I regain these natural gifts?" I asked.

"You must recognize them," she answered. "You never completely lost anything. You just buried those gifts way down deep inside you. You must recognize them and bring them back to the forefront of your being before I will become enjoyable to you again.

"Music lessons were not enjoyable to you as a child because you could already play. Your Music teacher forced you to play scales, fingerings, and rudiments but did not allow you to play freely, and that, you felt, held you back. Therefore you did not enjoy or benefit from those lessons. You approached each lesson with a sense of dread.

"Even now you feel that way about practicing. You don't want to practice; you just want to play. So if you feel that practice is necessary, it would benefit you to figure out how to practice while you play so that you can make the most of both. You have not been smart enough to figure that out yet. But know this: As your days approach their final numbers, you will not spend one moment wondering whether you've practiced your bass enough."

Thinking about my final days was a bit disturbing, but I knew that what she said was true. I would never again allow myself to waste precious time worrying about something as trivial as practicing. Even though I understood the benefits, I knew that practicing never took me as far as when I would allow myself to completely *let go* while playing Music. I loved that feeling, but it only happened on rare occasions. How could I make it a frequent occurrence? Music responded to my thoughts.

"In your mind, Music is not a part of who you are. It is something you have to go somewhere else to do. Whether it is the 'woodshed' or the nightclub, you feel that you must go to that place to find me. You do not carry me inside you at all times the way you once did. Actually, there are few who do anymore. This lack of union is causing me to die."

"I will work on it, I promise."

"It does not take work; it takes remembering, enjoying, rejoicing, recognizing, playing, and knowing. It should be easy. When you were a child it did not feel like work, and it should not feel like work now. If it does, you know you are going about it the wrong way. At that time, take a moment to go 'inside.' Remember what I truly feel like. Then you will know where to be and what to do next.

"Regain your knowing of me. Books and teachers can be of assistance but you should never let them take the place of what you feel and what you know within yourself. Only use these outside aids as tools to confirm, challenge, or show you more about what you know and feel inside. That is all. Never let them take the place of your natural gifts."

What she was saying was true, and I knew it. There was a time when our connection was so natural that I didn't have to think about it. I knew that was one of the gifts she was talking about.

"Give me five words to describe me," I felt her say.

As strange as it was, having a conversation with Music herself, I accepted it completely. And now she was asking me to describe her. Feeling her energy all around me, it was an easy task.

"Love. Emotion. Beauty. Expression. Harmony. Communication. Spiritual. Natural. Vibrations. God! I know I gave you more than five but I feel like I could go on forever."

"Yes, you could go on forever, and all of your words would be wonderful. The words you gave are beautiful ones that describe me perfectly. That should remind you that you *do* know who I am. Why is it then, that when it is time for you to play, you choose to forget?"

I didn't know what to think or say.

"Notice," she continued, "that you didn't choose the words technique, scales, modes, theory, notes, tapping, thumbing, major, minor, or key signatures. You didn't even use the words bass or guitar. But those are the words you choose to think about when it's time for you to play. Inside, you know that that's not who I really am. If all your attention is directed toward those words, when will you ever get to play Music? I suggest you take a good look at the wonderful words you used to describe me and learn how to play them. If that is what I am to you, that is what you should be playing.

"You have spent years learning how to play the bass, so long that you have forgotten that it is Music you should be playing. The bass is just a tool to help you express yourself through me. Why then, after all these years, do you continue to focus on the tool? You have forgotten. I patiently await your return."

Her vibrations pierced my flesh in a way that made me feel both guilty and refreshed. I knew she wasn't judging me, just telling the truth. The fact that she spoke through energy, not words, caused me to hear her with my whole body. And these vibrations were exactly what I needed; they seemed to touch my very soul.

"If you wanted to know more about your mother," she continued, "would you get a book and read about her? Would you find a teacher to teach you about her? A book might help you find your mother, but once you did find her, would you worship the book? Would you even need the book anymore? Or would you go directly to your mother and talk to her, listen to her, experience her, and unite with her? You and I both know the answer. Experiencing your mother directly would be the absolute best way for you to learn about her.

"Pertaining to Music, most people choose the first two methods because that is all they know. They don't realize they can do the latter. They talk about me as if they know me. They write books about me. They open schools that teach about me. They create whole departments in universities named after me. They even create and use numerous methods to play me, only to argue about which ones are best. And most of the time, it is only the superficial me they talk about, not the real me they once knew in their hearts. Can you believe they've actually turned me into a business?"

I could feel her power as she spoke, but then, as I continued to listen, her voice became so enchanting that it gave me goose bumps. "Goose bumps never lie," my mom always told me.

"What people don't do anymore is talk to me, simply and honestly talk to me," Music continued. "The few who do don't expect me to answer. My relationship with computers is about to become more intimate than it is with humans.

"People refuse to feel me. I reach out to them, but they retract their hands. That saddens me deeply. I tell you, it is a lonely world I live in. All I ask is to be felt. I reached out to you, and you took my hand. That makes me happy. You give me hope."

I felt sad for her. I could feel all her emotions seeping into me. It made me cry. I made a silent vow to remember that feeling and use it to help me change my ways. I realized once again that Music is real, alive, and approachable. I could talk with her, sit with her, embrace her, laugh, and cry with her. I also knew that I didn't have to try to create her anymore. She already exists. All I have to do is come to this place, and Music will be waiting, complete, whole, and alive.

I wanted to help others know what I knew. I wanted others to feel what I felt. I wanted to help others remember their union with Music in a real way. I would do my best to help keep her alive. I would no longer be a part of the death of Music.

"Thank you," I cried. "Thank you so much. You've helped me understand the responsibility, honor, and joy of being a musician."

"You are quite welcome, but you should also thank your bass. The instrument you have chosen helps you come to me on a daily basis. In all your musical years, when have you ever truthfully said 'thank you' to your bass guitar?"

The question stunned me. There was nothing I could say. She paused, allowing me time to digest her words before she continued.

"Do that honestly and frequently and notice what happens. All the elements that make up your instrument are alive. Your recognition and appreciation of them may change the way you respond to each other."

Thank my bass. It was a profound concept and I couldn't stop thinking about it. I found it hard to believe that I'd never done it before. I'd never even thought about it. After all the years of playing the instrument, I'd never once said "thank you" to it. I knew that some things in my life would have to change.

"Remember," she said, "play me all you want, but you must know this: it is only when you allow *me* to play *you* that you will know me completely because then we will be one and the same."

Allow Music to play me? That was another new concept that made complete sense. I didn't know why I hadn't thought of it before. I realized for the first time that my relationship with Music had always been one-sided. I'd never really listened to her. That type of relationship never worked.

"Only through the power of listening can you truly know anything," she told me.

Those words continue to stick with me.

Closing my eyes, I allowed her to take control. It caused a shift in my energy and for the first time I could sense my body. Something was growing inside me. It felt as if my whole body was vibrating with intense speed. I also noticed that I was glowing with vibrant colors, the same colors that Music was emanating. Music and I were becoming *one*. As good as it felt, I didn't trust myself enough to let go completely. I was still holding on to something.

Relax. Let go. What are you holding on to?

As soon as that thought entered my mind, I had a quick glimpse of myself, as the bag lady pushing the cart.

I fought hard to hold on to the feeling of light, the feeling of union, the feeling of—Music. I was losing it.

"Help me! What should I do?"

"There are no shoulds or shouldn'ts. There are only choices. What you choose to do next is up to you. No one can tell you what that is. You have been shown all you need to know."

I recognized the voice. I opened my tear-filled eyes to see Michael standing in front of me in the exact place he'd stood when he first appeared in my house. Was it he, or was it Music who'd been talking to me just moments ago?

For the first time since I'd met him, Michael was dressed in ordinary clothing. He wore black slacks, a button-down white shirt, and a tie. Even his shoes were normal, and there was no sign of his skateboard. I couldn't believe it. I was confused. "I must be dreaming," I said out loud.

Sitting up to get a better look, I shook my head and wiped the tears from my eyes. As they cleared, a change took place. Michael now appeared to be wearing the blue NASA-style jumpsuit I'd originally seen him in. In one hand was his motorcycle helmet. His skateboard was in the other.

"Michael!" was all I could think to say. Even though he now looked like himself, I was confused even more.

"Dress and act ordinary and you produce ordinary students," was all I heard him say.

With a quick smile and a wink of his eye, he was gone. Just gone. I didn't understand. I shook my head once more to see if it would make him reappear. It didn't. I couldn't figure out how to feel or what to think. The only thing I did know was that it would be the last time I would see him. I fell back on the couch, staring into space, clutching my bass in my lap.

I glanced across the room and saw a skateboard on the floor. I sat up. *Michael's*, I thought, *or . . . wait a minute, is it mine? I used to own one.* I reclined once again. I couldn't begin to figure it out. My mind was racing and I started to feel dizzy. I searched for it, but the line that separated asleep from awake was nowhere to be found, and the line that kept me sane was fading fast. I was losing it and I knew it. I was scared.

Pull yourself together, I told myself. *Don't get trapped by your mind.*

Wait a minute! I remember those words. They were Michael's. Or were they mine?

"Wake up! Go to sleep! Do something! Just don't lose it," I uttered aloud. "Michael warned me about this. Yes! Michael! Right! Think! What else did Michael say?"

You have been shown all you need to know.

Who said that? What did it mean? All I need to know to

do what? I still had no gigs, no money, and, if I didn't soon pay my rent, I'd have no place to live. My impending situation caused reality to creep in. That was a feeling I could handle. As if drowning in the sea, I grasped for that piece of reality like a Life preserver. I missed. Instead, I was drowning in the depths of my mind.

I tried hard to make sense out of any of it, but I couldn't even get myself off the couch. It was hard to believe that just a few moments earlier I was filled with emotion and tears, and now I was scared and depressed. I tried to go back to sleep, but couldn't.

Maybe I am asleep. Wait a minute, have I been asleep all along? I just sat down to practice, right?

I shook my head again and struggled to get up. In the process, I accidentally plucked a string on my bass guitar. With the bass lying in my lap, the sound reverberated through my body triggering a familiar feeling. I was starting to regain some composure.

I thought about Music. The thought of her caused me to relax a bit more. I focused harder, trying to see if I could reclaim more of my mind. It worked. I could remember part of my vision and vow to help keep her alive, but I couldn't remember how I was supposed to do it.

Remember! You can do it, I told myself. *Try harder.*

I lay there thinking hard enough to make my head hurt when I heard Michael's voice, one more time.

Try easy, my friend. Try easy.

Back to the Beginning

What is more dangerous to a person: success or failure?

L ife has a way of repeating itself. It also seems to go by much faster as one gets older. It's been nearly five years since I pushed that shopping cart, and even though I can sometimes hear his voice in my head and can still recall every experience like it happened yesterday, I haven't seen Michael since that day. Well, actually, I'm not so sure about that.

Last summer, I was invited to play a benefit concert at Carnegie Hall in New York City, which was a thrill, to say the least. While playing, I thought I saw a familiar face sitting in the balcony. I felt him more than I saw him. Maybe I just wanted it to be him.

The balcony at that theater is too far away to clearly see

anyone's face, but when he winked at me, I was pretty sure that it was him. There was an unmistakable sparkle that I recognized. As far as I know, he didn't leave a note or try to make contact with me in any other way. It would be good to see him again, but I don't expect to, though I do continue to think and dream about him. Somehow I feel that he is somewhere close, watching.

Much has changed in the last five years, and because of Michael, my Life is continually changing for the better. My relationship with Music is allowing me to play better than ever and everyone can tell. It took me a while, but now I think I understand what it meant when I was told that I needed to stop playing the instrument. These days, even though I'm not yet consistent, I do my best to play Music instead of the bass.

I've become a regular member of Jonell's band and continue to play with The Cliffnotes when time allows. I feel fortunate that staying busy and keeping my head above water is no longer a struggle.

Recently, I heard about a bluegrass musician who is forming a jazz band to perform a few songs on a television show. He heard about me through a mutual friend and wants me to contact him. I'm not sure if my style will work with his. My taste for bluegrass hasn't fully developed yet, but since he's putting together a jazz band, I may give him a call.

Being recognized and sought out by local musicians has done a lot for my self esteem. When the local Music Society awarded me the honor of Nashville Bass Player of the Year, it came as a surprise. The second time, even though I sort of expected it, was still a great honor and has led to other opportunities.

The recognition of my peers makes me feel wonderful, and I appreciate all of it, but I'm always sure to keep myself in check. "What is more dangerous to a person: success or failure?" Michael once asked me. I know people who have been hurt on both sides of that fence. A few acquaintances of mine were almost unrecognizable after they had achieved success. They turned into people I never would've chosen as friends. A few others gave up after just a few failures, allowing their lifelong dreams to dissipate. I decided to do my best not to fall into either of those categories.

I'm now also being asked by Music stores and colleges to teach master classes and clinics. I don't consider myself a master of anything, nor do I have much class, but even though I never attended college, I guess I do have a few things to offer.

People repeatedly ask me which Music schools I've attended. Michael's School of Music and Life, I'm always tempted to say, but never have. I haven't told many people about my experiences with him. Even my girlfriend hasn't heard the whole story. I am always willing to share the lessons learned but rarely do I tell anyone where I learned them.

Who would believe me anyway? I mean, I never found out who Michael really was or where he came from. The more time goes by, the more I start to think that maybe, just maybe, he came from my imagination, from some unused portion of my mind, where he's now gone back to live again. I can still hear him knocking around in there much of the time. Like I said, it's as if he's constantly rearranging the furniture.

I think about all of them a lot: Michael, Uncle Clyde, Sam, and Isis. Why were these bizarre people sent to me? Or was I sent to them? Either way, the short time we spent together brought me further along the path of Music than I ever could've imagined.

You see to me, they are Music. It was made clear to me that Music is related to everything, especially nature and language, but in order to speak it naturally, I had to first make myself a part of it. Music herself told me that, and now that I understand what she was talking about, I can fully appreciate the lyric, "I once was lost, but now am found."

Now regarding Isis: I don't know which was stranger—her or her information. Anyway, it's taken me nearly five years, but now I can clearly see the part numbers play in Music. All Music can be broken down into numbers, and since Music and Life are the same, I guess that Life is numbers too. I once heard someone say that all of Life could be broken down into a mathematical equation. That's too much math for me, but I guess anything is possible. I *do* know that Nashville musicians have figured out a way to read and write Music without using letters at all. They call it the Nashville Number System.

Sam and I are now constant companions. He's the only one with whom I can share Michael stories. We hang out together and help each other assimilate all that we're still learning. Although I've progressed enough to be able to show him a few things, Sam still does most of the teaching.

Uncle Clyde died a few years ago. At least that's what I think happened. It made me think about a saying I once heard Michael use. It had something to do with a library being lost every time an elderly person dies. That definitely applies to Clyde. I know that I'd only gotten a glimpse of the knowledge inside his mind.

I used to visit him regularly until one day he and his few belongings were gone. When I asked people in the area about him, no one seemed to know who I was talking about. A few people said they remembered something about a car accident. Maybe it was the one I witnessed; the one where Michael and Clyde's help brought a man back to Life. I seemed to be the only one who had a clear recollection of the man who lived under the bridge. That was strange, but there was something more bizarre than that.

When I went to visit Clyde for the last time, there was nothing left under the bridge except his harmonica. It was sitting there out in the open, apparently waiting for me. I was surprised that no one had taken it. Michael would've said that Clyde left it for me, and I'm sure that Clyde would've wanted me to have it. So I took it. I was sad that day.

The most peculiar part of the story lies in the fact that when I picked up his harp, I could play it. When I first touched it, I knew I could play it, so I did. Right then and there, all by myself, I played. When I returned home and took out Clyde's instrument, the feeling wasn't there, so I didn't attempt to play it again and haven't since. I know that I'll regain the feeling when the time is right.

A similar thing happened with Isis. After getting a better

handle on what she had talked about, I went back to the bookstore to ask her more questions. To my surprise, there were no signs of her anywhere in the store. Even her table was gone. The sales clerk told me that they didn't offer gift-wrapping and never had. Feeling unsure of myself, I didn't ask if Isis had ever worked there.

When I returned to my car there was a blank card stuck under the left windshield wiper. When I pulled the card out and flipped it over, I was shocked. There was nothing on it but a handwritten circle. *The number zero.*

I was bewildered. I wandered all around the parking lot looking for Isis. *She couldn't have gotten far.* I listened for the jingle of her bells. There was nothing. I started to go back into the store to ask more questions, but something told me to just let it be.

Tired, dazed, and confused, I got in the car. As I cranked the engine, a song by the Beatles just happened to be playing on the radio. Paul McCartney's lyrics eased my mind as his soothing voice filled the air: "Let it be."

I did just that. And I keep that card in my wallet at all times.

Believe it or not, I've also kept in touch with the red shouldered hawk. Or maybe it's he who has kept in touch with me. He's chosen to follow me since I moved to the woods west of town. The nest he shares with his bride is just a short walk from my log cabin. Whenever I get that certain feeling, I go outside and he's usually sitting there on a low limb. I just watch him stare at me, tilting his head from side to side. He acts as if he has something to tell me, or maybe he's just checking up on me. Although I try, I haven't gotten him to land on my arm yet. Maybe one day.

Following Michael's instruction, I've started meditating every day. Well, almost every day. It has really helped me in all aspects of my Life, especially with my connection to Music and the natural world. I've also become a fairly decent naturalist and tracker. I attribute most of it to daily meditation.

Things are really going well now that I've processed most of what Michael has shown me. His lessons and concepts were relatively simple to grasp once I was made aware of them. I also had to become familiar with his teaching style. For example: When he first told me that notes were overrated, I didn't quite understand what he was getting at. I found out later that he didn't actually believe that statement. He'd told me that just to make me focus more on the other elements. He felt, as I now do, that the other elements are neglected by most teachers and musicians and that they need more attention. I finally understand it.

His stretching-the-truth style of teaching was new to me, but once I understood how and why it was used, I added it to my own teaching method.

Awareness was also an integral part of his teachings, and it's become a part of mine. He made me aware of things that I'd never thought about. Now that I've tuned in to his way of thinking, I've made it my own and produce my own miracles.

One day while I was in an art museum in Paris, a strange

thing happened. I noticed a string of faint but glowing tracks on the marble floor. I'd never seen tracks like those, so I did what any tracker would've done; I followed them. They led me to a kid who'd been separated from his parents. He told me that he'd stopped to look at something, and when he turned around, they were gone. His tears were almost too much for me to bear. I found an employee and told her what was going on. That led to a quick and happy reunion with his family. The incident wasn't as strange as the fact that the whole thing took place in French. I'd never spoken French until that moment.

It was later that I remembered getting the tingling feeling when I saw the boy's tears. It was the same feeling I get every time I sense the hawk or when I picked up Uncle Clyde's harmonica and realized I could play it. The feeling is still kind of surreal. Like a premonition, it always precedes the experience. Whenever it shows up, I know that something special is soon to follow. I finally understand my childhood attraction to Spider Man. It's as if I have my very own spidey sense.

When I returned from Paris it started happening all the time. I would just know things without knowing where the knowledge came from. At first it surprised me, but now I expect it. This confidence makes it come on even stronger. Every time it happens, I joke with myself that it's Michael inside my head.

Thanking my bass is a new habit of mine. I used to give thanks only when I was about to eat a meal, but now I say "thank you" to everything. I thank my headaches, my clothes, my television, and my Life. And I thank Music. I thank everything all the time, and it really makes a difference.

The first time I really thanked my bass was an amazing experience. The whole concept was new to me. I wasn't sure what I was supposed to do, but I poured myself into it.

I thanked the tuning pegs for enduring the heat as they were being melted down. I thanked the strings for being wound and twisted. I thanked the wood for being cut, scraped, and sanded. I thanked the wires, the pickups, the electronics, and batteries. I even thanked the people and thoughts involved in manufacturing each part. I thanked everything I could think of for going through what it went through in order to produce an instrument for my benefit. I also apologized for not doing so before. The whole process took about twenty minutes.

Once I was finished, I stood up, put my guitar in its case, and picked up my other bags. As I bent down to pick up my bass, it seemed to lift itself and fly over my shoulder. I stood there in shock. Usually the case alone is enough to give me a backache, but that time it felt as light as a feather. *Aw man Michael, this stuff really works.*

The strangest of all coincidences happened while I was visiting my parents in Virginia. I was in between tours and had decided to go back to my hometown for a few days of vacation. While I was there I made contact with many old friends and spent some quality time with my folks.

I decided, for some reason, to go out jogging early one morning. When I got outside I realized that it was a bit chillier than I thought; I hadn't dressed appropriately. The sun had not yet risen enough to warm the day. Running was not my favorite hobby, and I was not about to run while cold.

Not wanting to waste any time, I went back to my parents' house to grab the first thing I could find to stay warm. Realizing that I'd locked myself out of their house, I grabbed my mom's yellow rain jacket off the porch and the wide-brimmed brown hat my dad used for gardening. Since my folks weren't up yet, I figured I could use the garments without them being missed. I realized that the clothes, along with my blue running tights, would make me a peculiar sight.

I ran further than I thought I would that morning. Not being an experienced jogger, I found myself exhausted, several miles from my parents' house. I'd forgotten that I would have to run back. I decided to walk.

On my way home, I decided to take a shortcut (or so I thought) through a department store parking lot. From a distance I noticed what looked like a unicycle leaning against the store's garbage Dumpster. Getting closer, I realized I was right. A longtime fan of the circus, I took the unicycle, planning to make it ride-able someday. The rim was bent, making the wheel wobble as I rolled it down the street.

The town had changed a lot since I was last there. That, coupled with the shortcut, had me thoroughly disoriented. Once I realized I was lost, *it* happened.

It started with the now-familiar tingle, which was stronger than usual that day. I didn't know what it was or what it meant, but I knew that something or someone was speaking to me. I heightened my awareness and sent out my feelers in every direction. Nothing stood out so I kept walking until I reached the next apartment complex. It was there that things started to feel familiar although nothing was recognizable.

As I walked by, I noticed a flash of light come from somewhere on the third floor of one of the buildings. I wondered if it was just a reflection from the sun. Unable to ignore it, I found myself walking up the stairs to the third floor, unicycle in tow.

Once I reached the area where the flash had come from, I noticed I was standing outside an apartment. The door was right in front of me. Don't ask me why, but I just walked right in.

As I entered the apartment I could immediately tell I was in a single man's home. Stuff was scattered everywhere. I looked across the room and noticed a young man in his early twenties sleeping on the couch with, you guessed it, an electric bass guitar in his lap.

Interesting. I walked over to get a closer look. As soon as I was standing in front of him, his eyes opened.

"Who are you?" he asked, maybe calmer than he should've been.

Not knowing what else to say, I went with my gut. "I am your teacher," I answered.

"Teacher of what?"

"Nothing."

"How'd you get in here?" he questioned.

"You asked me to come."

"I did? Did I give you a key?"

"I don't need a key."

"What are you gonna teach me?"

"Nothing."

"What do you mean 'nothing'?"

"Exactly that. Nothing. I can teach you nothing because no one can teach anybody anything. But I can *show* you things."

"Can you show me music?" he asked.

"Yes I can, but not as well as Music herself can show you."

"What do you mean 'music herself'?"

"You'll see, or not," I answered, sporting a Cheshire-cat grin of my own.

"If you're not a teacher, who are you and what do I call you?"

I thought before I answered. I could've told him anything. "Victor," I said. "Call me Victor."

He sat up on the edge of the couch. "Okay, Victor, let's get started then."

Wow, he's already much further along than I was. I wasn't sure if I was as ready as my new student seemed to be.

Then I realized what was happening. For the first time I fully understood what Michael was getting at when he told me something about being the "keeper of the flame."

"Remember," Michael had said, "it is easy to learn to play your instrument, but playing it well is not enough. It is time for you to enter the world of a true musician. It is time for you to become an ally of Music and share her blessings. You are now the keeper of the flame. Please keep that flame alive and do not, I say, *do not* allow Music to die."

What am I getting myself into? I'm not Michael. This is his gig, not mine. But I was there and he wasn't. So I decided to go with it. What else was I to do?

As I started to take a seat, I glanced down at myself, realizing what I must look like. "Dress and act ordinary, and you produce ordinary students," were the words that came to mind. I decided, at that moment, to do my best to live up to that statement.

Michael would be proud. Playing with that kid's mind was already fun, and I was looking forward to more.

Accepting my new role I took my seat, pulled the brim down over my eyes, and held the unicycle in my lap. Sitting poised and ready, I prepared to strum the spokes.

"Where do you want to begin?" I asked the kid.

As he sat up in his chair, an all-too-familiar phrase was spoken:

"Boy, do I have a lot to learn!"

About the Author

Victor Lemonte Wooten is a four-time Grammy Award–winning musician and a three-time winner of *Bass Player* magazine's Player of the Year award (the only bass player to win this award more than once).

The youngest of five brothers, he started playing the bass guitar around the age of two and was the bass player in the family band, The Wooten Brothers, before he started school. Victor credits his brothers and his parents for his outlook on Music and Life.

His unique gifts as well as his love for sharing them inspired writer Paul Hargett to write an authorized biography about him titled *Me and My Bass Guitar* (Amberock Publications, www.meandmy bassguitar.com).

He continues to record and tour with his own band and as an original member of the Grammy Award–winning ensemble Béla Fleck & the Flecktones.

Victor lives with his wife and four kids in a log cabin near Nashville, Tennessee.

To find out more about Victor Lemonte Wooten, his Music, his Music books, his camps, and other interests, please visit:

www.victorwooten.com
www.thebassvault.com
www.flecktones.com